~

THIS ISLAND IN TIME

~

This Island in Time

REMARKABLE TALES FROM
MONTREAL'S PAST

John Kalbfleisch

Véhicule Press

Published with the generous assistance of The Canada Council for
the Arts, the Book Publishing Industry Development Program of the
Department of Canadian Heritage and the Société de développement des
entreprises culturelles du Québec (SODEC).

Cover design: J.W. Stewart
Cover image: *Nelson's Monument, Notre-Dame Street Looking West*
by Robert Auchmuty Sproule, 1830.
Frontispiece: Nuns walk in the garden of the Hospitalières de Saint-
Joseph, Hôtel-Dieu, Montreal, c. 1908. (Photographer unknown,
Archives of the Hospitalières de Saint-Joseph.)
Special thanks to David LeBlanc
Set in Adobe Minion and Adobe Caslon by Simon Garamond
Printed by Marquis Book Printing Inc.

Copyright © John Kalbfleisch 2008

Dépôt légal, Bibliothèque nationale du Québec and
the National Library of Canada, third trimester 2008

LIBRARY AND ARCHIVES CANADA CATALOGUING IN PUBLICATION

Kalbfleisch, John, 1943-
This island in time : remarkable tales from Montreal's
past / John Kalbfleisch.
Includes index.

ISBN 978-1-55065-241-3

1. Montréal (Québec)—Biography. 2. Montréal (Québec)—History.
I. Title.

FC2947.4.K34 2008   971.4'280099   C2007-907372-7

Published by Véhicule Press, Montréal, Québec, Canada
www.vehiculepress.com

Distribution in Canada by LitDistCo
orders@litdistco.ca

Distribution in U.S. by Independent Publishers Group
www.ipgbook.com

Printed in Canada on 100% post-consumer recycled paper.

Je vous envoye …cette relation afin qu'elle vous serve d'un vaisseau fort commode pour venir au Montréal.

[I send you this account … in order that it may serve you as a most convenient ship in which to come to Montreal.]

–François Dollier de Casson, 1672

Contents

Preface

Anyone who proposes to write history but who, like me, has no formal training as a historian must especially rely on the work of others. Fortunately, Montreal throughout its long history has been unusually blessed with witnesses to its passage through time.

Repeatedly, librarians have shown me the way to interesting stories from Montreal's past. It is unfashionable, even dangerous, to make sweeping declarations about classes of people. With librarians, however, I have no hesitation in making such a claim: they are interested in people every bit as much as they are in books, and are unfailingly efficient and cheerful. Those whom I've met while writing this book, without exception, have pitched in whenever I've approached them—and with a smile as well.

In particular, I must acknowledge the assistance of Pat Duggan and Liz Ferguson of *The Gazette's* library in Montreal. Not once have they blanched when I have called on them for help in confirming even the most trivial or obscure of details.

I am also deeply in debt to the staff of Library and Archives Canada in Ottawa. I have haunted their reading rooms for several years now, and have presented myself countless times to their inquiry desks. Nonetheless, and to my shame, I still know none of them by name; nor surely have I been, to them, anything but an anonymous member of the public. Yet simply being one more person interested in learning something is, for them, all that matters. I'm confident they have treated me with the same thoroughness and good will that researchers far better known than I am would expect as a matter of course. What a wonderful treasure Canadians have in this institution and its people.

I am extremely fortunate to have known the late Edgar Andrew Collard, for a time even to have worked in the office next to his. His *Gazette* columns and his many books on what he called "the days that are no more" have opened a unique door on the personal and the intimate. Any writer proposing, like me, to step through that door will always be in his debt. I am also indebted to Michael Goldbloom and Peter Hadekel, respectively the publisher and editorial-page editor of *The Gazette* at the time, for inviting me to take over the newspaper's Montreal history column following Collard's death in 2000. The writing of that column has been an invaluable preparation for this book.

I would be remiss if I did not record how I have benefited from the enthusiasm for Montreal's history that flows from my *Gazette* colleague Alan Hustak. I am grateful to John Angus of Beaconsfield, Quebec, who pointed me toward Charlie McCormick. Professor Jonathan Wagner of Minot State University in North Dakota kindly helped to unravel the enigma of Karl Gerhard. I have been guided through some thickets of seventeenth-century French prose by my brother-in-law Dale Bjorgan.

Finally, I must thank my immediate family. My daughters, Catherine and Elizabeth, have been a constant inspiration in ways they cannot know. My wife, Cecelia McGuire, has always been on hand while I was writing to offer gentle sympathy or stern-minded resolve, as the situation demanded, to say nothing of her remarkable skills as an editor. Here, as in so much else, I would have been lost without her. I unreservedly dedicate *This Island in Time* to her, and to the memory of my parents, Isa Taylor and William Kalbfleisch.

A Note on Style

Since everything in this book took place before the 1970s, when the metric system came to Canada in earnest, I have not hesitated to retain old imperial units like the pound and the mile.

In quotations from old sources, I have occasionally—and silently—modernized the punctuation to make the meaning clearer.

With the names of people, I have used the forms most familiar to readers of English. Thus, the founder of Montreal, Paul de Maisonneuve, is de Maisonneuve in subsequent references, but the founder of Quebec City, Samuel de Champlain, is merely Champlain. In cases where several versions of a name exist, I have let the *Dictionary of Canadian Biography* be my guide, as with Luc de La Corne de Saint-Luc.

I have chosen to use modern place names. However, a big exception is context where an older, probably English version was once in common use—St. James Street instead of Rue Saint-Jacques—or where, even today, such a version remains more familiar to most English-speakers—Sherbrooke Street instead of Rue Sherbrooke, or the St. Lawrence River rather than le Fleuve Saint-Laurent.

That is why, too, this book is not about Montréal but rather Montreal.

Introduction

In Montreal many years ago, a man who worked in an office on what was then called St. James Street was visited by his son. The son, who was twenty-one, had been studying in western Canada and was not especially familiar with the city where his parents had moved a couple of years before. It was around mid-day. The two slipped out into the busy street, and in a matter of minutes they were in Place d'Armes. They paused a moment to take it all in: the muscular bulk of Notre Dame Church, the Sulpician seminary almost twice as old, doughty de Maisonneuve on his granite column, the oddly compelling Bank of Montreal beneath its low dome, and finally the people scurrying in all directions.

The older man was my father, and though he might have lacked a gift for imaginative words, he did not lack for imagination itself. "Look at it," he said to me. "What stories it all could tell."

What stories, indeed. Europeans have made their homes on Montreal's island longer than almost anywhere else you'd care to name in the country. Amerindians have been there much longer. For most of the time that there's been a Montreal, the city has been the country's largest and most important. No wonder it is the fulcrum of Canada's history, the place where, more than any other, people have arrived, have rubbed up against each other and in some cases have moved on, so many of them helping to shape the nation we know today. In this sense, Montreal is the country's true capital.

What follows in this book is the telling of stories. Here, you will not find history as it is usually written, with its ordered succession of events, each leading more or less inevitably to the next, with great—or sometimes not so great—figures moving across the page doing remarkable things as they go. Instead, the focus will be more modest, often on people you might not have heard of acting in special ways, or people you doubtless have heard of acting in ways that wouldn't fit comfortably into more formal history books.

In October 2000, I began to write *The Gazette*'s Montreal history column—only later would the newspaper move away from Old Montreal —and it was a repeated delight to be able to step from the door, on what's now Rue Saint-Jacques, and see across the street, scarcely a stone's throw away, the very windows of my father's old office, where doubtless he once pondered some of the stories I now tell.

My column is called "Second Draft." I chose that label as a nod to the late Philip Graham, publisher of the *Washington Post*, who once said that newspapers give us the first rough draft of history. Every day, reporters, columnists and photographers record political manoeuvrings and business failures, bank robberies and terrorist attacks, show-business follies and hockey scores. It's often done on the fly—the pressure of daily deadlines ensures that—and in their rush to record the who or the what, journalists sometimes miss the who-else or the why.

Mind you, there are virtues in the headlong rush to meet a deadline, chief among them the protection that rush gives against making hasty, half-baked assumptions about the significance of it all. There often simply is no time to be profound. Reporters above all else report; they are "strangers to omniscience," as John Carey of Oxford University has put it. In his wonderful book *Eyewitness to History*, Carey writes that with reporters, "the varnish of interpretation has been removed so we can see people clearly, as they originally were."

Those old newspaper accounts are certainly not history as most professional historians would care to write it, though historians are not so foolish as to deny their worth. As Carey implies, it is the journalist of the moment who has actually seen and heard and smelled what historians years or even centuries later can often only guess at.

Imagine if you will the clay pot carried by a child a millennium ago on the slopes of what we now call Mount Royal. It was a fine day, and in a moment of inattention the pot fell to the ground. It shattered; the child was scolded; and the incident was soon forgotten. After all, the child was well loved and there were many other pots in the village. But the shard from that pot that an archaeologist might find today would be far from trivial. Its shape, the minute traces of the pot's contents, the hint of colouring it bore, and the precise spot where it was found would be potent clues to life in what might—or might not—have been Hochelaga.

Something similar applies to Graham's first drafts of history. A brief, three-sentence item about a carthorse that unaccountably bolted, leaving the driver badly injured and the barrels of fresh water he was delivering tumbled into the street, would be interesting, though familiar, news to a newspaper reader 150 years ago. But for anyone coming across that brief account today, it has the power to evoke a whole range of notions now alien to us, everything from the dangers of working with animals to the sketchiness of nineteenth-century medical care and the difficulty of keeping something potable to drink in the house.

There is nothing unusual about keeping the story in Montreal's history. *The Gazette*'s Edgar Andrew Collard did precisely that in a weekly column that ran without interruption for an astonishing fifty-six years, until just a few weeks before his death in the summer of 2000. In his very first column, on August 14, 1944, Collard flatly rejected any claim to being a historian and was proud, instead, to assume the less honoured mantle of antiquarian. And why should he not have been proud? Here, in part, is what he wrote that day:

"The antiquarian ... can claim with justice that he, and not the historian, is nearer to the substance of historical reality. For human experience is, after all, a matter of details. True, it is possible to stand off from life and to generalize from historical facts, as from statistics. The results may be extremely valuable. But where in this broad analysis is the day-to-day quality that makes up human experience?"

Those first drafts of history in *The Gazette* are vital for providing the stories that now appear in my Second Draft column. Heaven knows, there are a lot of first drafts: the newspaper was founded well over two centuries ago, on June 3, 1778. Each column reflects a search in *The Gazette*'s archives for something of the day-to-day quality that fascinated Collard, "those significant details," as he put it, "that lie so near to the mysterious heart of human life."

But old newspapers, of course, are not the only time machines that can help whisk us back to an earlier Montreal. Newspaper reporters are not the only people who report. Other sources help in the search for that "mysterious heart" of Montreal.

In the *Jesuit Relations* for 1642, for example, Father Barthélemy Vimont describes the Feast of the Assumption on August 15, not yet three months after Montreal was founded. In it is the first recorded reference to a crude chapel that would eventually evolve into the vast church in Place d'Armes where my father and I would pause more than three centuries later:

"The fine tabernacle sent out by the Gentlemen was placed upon the Altar of a Chapel which, as yet, is built only of bark, but which is nonetheless valuable. The good Souls who were there received communion. ... The thunder of the cannons caused the whole island to re-echo, and the Demons, although accustomed to thunderbolts, were frightened by a voice that spoke of the love that we bear to the great Mistress. ... After the instruction given to the Savages, there was a fine Procession after Vespers, in which those good people took part, quite astonished at seeing so pious a ceremony."

Or consider this description of a huge raft of timbers coming down the St. Lawrence near Montreal, a sight once so common as to be almost banal. Here's what James Thomson, an immigrant baker about twenty-two years old, said in a letter to his father back in Scotland in June 1844:

"You will think it no great wonder after all when I tell you it was only a float of wood coming down the water, but it was none of your Water of Dee floats with Sandy Rae on one end and John Michie on the other. It was an immense field of floating timbers, the logs squared and built one upon another I don't know how deep. There were a dozen masts upon it with a sail on each, a great many men with wooden houses and fires, and the whole pulled along by a steamer."

Just as vivid is the recollection by Francis Shepherd, the distinguished surgeon and medical reformer, of operations at the Montreal General Hospital when he was studying medicine more than 130 years ago:

"In cases of bad compound fracture of the leg, the limb was amputated, for if left alone the patient was sure to die of sepsis, while he had a chance with amputation. Many of the operators were very skilful, especially in amputation; they never made a mistake in the flaps; rapid operating was the rule. I have not infrequently seen an amputation of the thigh completed in less than one minute. ... It was thought to be most dangerous to tie a vein. It was usually closed by a piece of muscle, or pressure was used. I remember in an operation on the neck having to tie the jugular, a proceeding which shocked an old surgeon who was present."

Young James Thomson found himself, in Carey's phrase, "gazing incredulously at what was, for that moment, the newest thing that had ever happened." And today, reading Thomson's account, and Vimont's and Shepherd's, we can share something of that same sense of wonder.

I must emphasize the book you now hold in your hands is not an anthology of Second Draft columns from the past several years. There are stories here that I've not tried to tell before. And when you do hear the echo of a column that has already appeared, I hope you'll find its story told in a new way, often making use of information that came to me since it appeared in *The Gazette* or that limitations of space forced me to do without.

Nor is there anything comprehensive about the ground this book covers. The chapter on street scenes is not a gazetteer of every street in Montreal, and the gallery of religious zealots does not include every fanatic who ever roiled the city's people. Rather the glimpses into another time are meant to be just that, glimpses.

Occasionally, these tales will seem to stray from Montreal—to the Gaspé, or to the United States, or even to China and Tibet—but while the ties that bind them to the city might stretch, they do not break.

As with the column, you will find nothing here that dates from later than Expo year. Simply to provide a kind of narrative end-point, and quite arbitrarily, I have told myself that nothing that's happened since 1967 is history.

Not yet. But it will be.

Chapter One

~

These are the names, the streets; the shorthand for the reality.
–Scott Symons, "Place d'Armes," 1967

In the beginning, there was a low-lying triangle of land. It was flanked by the St. Lawrence River, by a small tributary called the Rivière Saint-Pierre and by marshy land behind. This was Pointe à Callières. The soil was not especially rich, and trees had had a hard time re-establishing themselves after Samuel de Champlain had cleared much of its few acres during a brief stay thirty-one years before. It was here, one bright day in May 1642, that Paul de Chomedey, Sieur de Maisonneuve, and his small party, perhaps four dozen souls in all, came ashore to establish Ville Marie, today's Montreal. Most of them were men, but there were four women among them, including the nurse Jeanne Mance, and even a few children.

This was to be no ordinary community. Their aim was not merely to settle the land but to convert the native Indians to Christianity. That very day, they set up a small altar by the shore and Father Barthélemy Vimont, their Jesuit priest, celebrated mass. "What you see is but a grain of mustard seed," he famously told them, "but it is sown by hands so pious and so moved by the spirit of faith and piety that … I have no doubt that this seed will grow into a great tree, one day to achieve wonders."

In the beginning, of course, there were no streets. A few paths were soon tramped into the ground, marking where the settlers ventured into the bush for the timber or game they needed, but that was all. A log palisade was erected to protect a handful of small buildings, including a rough chapel. Like the boggy ground behind them, the waters of the two rivers, one mighty, one scarcely more than a creek, seemed to offer additional protection. But these same waters would soon present grave danger instead.

One day, with their first Christmas almost upon them, the French were greeted by a sudden thaw. The rivers rose quickly and soon were lapping at the palisade. If they rose much further, they could ruin Ville Marie's food and gunpowder, perhaps even drive the settlers away from their shelter entirely and out into the open. That would spell disaster.

De Maisonneuve was not dismayed. How could he be, with his unshakable faith in God? He set up a small cross at the edge of the fast-approaching water, and to it he affixed a document drawn up by his own hand. He "beseeched His Divine Majesty to hold the waters in their normal place" and promised that if Ville Marie were spared he would erect a much larger cross, a testament to God's mercy, on the mountain-side behind them.

Father Vimont recorded what happened next. "Just at midnight, and just as we were celebrating the birth of the Son of God on Earth," the waters began to recede.

A few days later, de Maisonneuve acted on his vow. He turned to Ville Marie's carpenter, Gilbert Barbier, a short, almost dwarf-like man known as Le Minime. Ordinarily the nickname would have been a disparaging one, but given the value of his skills it was probably used more with affection than in mockery. Le Minime fashioned a wooden cross, not so massive that it could not be carried on one man's shoulder, but still imposing enough that it could be seen from a distance. By January 6, the Feast of the Epiphany, all was ready. A line of pilgrims, de Maisonneuve prominent among them, burdened by the cross, set out from the little fort.

We don't know their exact route, though perhaps from time to time they followed the line of some street that Montrealers walk today. In any case, the going must have been difficult, soggy in parts, perhaps snow-clogged elsewhere. Branches would have to be cleared away, fallen tree trunks avoided. Indeed, a recent historian of that early time, Patricia Simpson, flatly states "a road (was) cleared." But even if, as seems more

Marguerite Bourgeoys opened Montreal's first school in a stable
in 1658.
(Painting attributed to William Von Mol Berczy, 1805, from the
Maison Saint-Gabriel collection.)

Indian girls were taught in one of the 17th-century stone towers
that survive to this day in front of the Grand Séminaire de
Montréal on Sherbrooke Street.
(Illustration from *L'Opinion Publique*, October 19, 1876.)

likely, a mere path was created instead of something like a street, the
liturgical procession that day was nothing less than street theatre—with
the settlers themselves and the God in whom they trusted the only
audience.

Father Vimont says they made it to "the highest crest" of the
mountain, perhaps to where the illuminated metal cross now shines
over the city to commemorate that faraway act of faith. But as Marguerite
Bourgeoys would later testify, a site of more modest height, a little above
Sherbrooke Street, rings truer. A simple altar of wood was assembled,
again thanks to Le Minime, and mass was celebrated.

Marguerite Bourgeoys wouldn't arrive in Ville Marie until ten years
later, in 1653. She came to the tiny settlement intending to found its first
school. By then, de Maisonneuve's cross had been destroyed by hostile
Indians, its pieces left scattered on the ground. She visited the site, saw
the cross's remains and resolved to erect a new one on the very spot.
This she did, ordering that wooden pickets also be put in place to
surround and protect it. Directing the working party was Le Minime.

At first, there were no children for Marguerite to teach, such had been the ravages of infant mortality. It was not until 1658, in an abandoned stone stable at Pointe à Callières, that her work began in earnest. In time, she and her companions found they could establish other schools elsewhere on the island as well. Their mission became formalized as the Congrégation de Notre Dame in 1672.

One of the satellite schools, especially dedicated to instructing Indian girls, was at a fort the Sulpicians had built on the slopes of Mount Royal to protect converts. It was a natural choice, for the fort was close to the spot hallowed by the two crosses that Le Minime had fashioned. At first the sisters taught in rough huts made from branches and bark. But sometime after 1685, the fort was reconstructed in stone, with four stout towers anchoring its walls. By the end of the century, the sisters had moved into two of the towers.

Those two towers have survived to this day. Passers-by on Sherbrooke Street can see them, on the grounds in front of the Grand Séminaire de Montréal. The tower to the left was the school, while the one to the right is where the sisters lived.

In 1672, François Dollier de Casson began his *Histoire de Montréal*. Rich in anecdote, it nonetheless is silent about any track that led to where the crosses were raised, even though it was already becoming a site of pilgrimage. But Dollier does record the existence of a very early *chemin de traîne*. This was a rough track over which timber was hauled to build a permanent hospital, the first Hôtel-Dieu, for Jeanne Mance. Without de Maisonneuve's Christmas promise to God, Ville Marie might never have seen its first birthday; without the existence of this *chemin de traîne*, it might never have seen its second.

Despite their escape late in 1642, de Maisonneuve's settlers soon concluded they would continue to be plagued with flooding at Pointe à Callières. The higher land across the Rivière Saint-Pierre began to beckon. That was the Coteau Saint-Louis, a low ridge running parallel to the St. Lawrence. That was where a proper hospital would soon start to rise, indeed where Ville Marie as a whole would grow.

But for the winter of 1643-44, they were still confined to the original site. Constant Iroquois raids made it dangerous to venture beyond the stockade. The close quarters, the inactivity, left them angry and frustrated, not least with de Maisonneuve who wouldn't allow them to sally out and confront their tormenters. "If we chase them as you desire," he told the men, "since we are but a handful, with little experience as bush fighters, we would immediately be surprised in an ambush where there'd be twenty Iroquois to one Frenchman." These were not comforting odds.

But when the men began to grumble that their leader was lacking in courage, de Maisonneuve decided he could not hold back much longer. Weakened morale might be just as great a threat to Ville Marie, in its own way, as the Indians.

The crunch came on the morning of March 30, 1644. The settlement's pack of dogs, led by the watchful Pilotte, scented a band of intruders across the Rivière Saint-Pierre. With the dogs yapping madly, and his men pressing him, de Maisonneuve decided to act. A small party would be left to guard the fort; the rest would go with him.

The snow lay deep, and only a few of the men had snowshoes. The rest struggled along as best they could. There were only about thirty of them, but they had firearms, to say nothing of the confidence their faith in God gave them.

Faith and firearms alike were tested shortly after they crossed the little river and entered the woods. Suddenly the Indians attacked, perhaps 200 of them. Just as de Maisonneuve had predicted, his men were badly outnumbered, and some of their adversaries had muskets of their own. Sheltering behind tree trunks, the French laid down fire as best they could, but the Indians remorselessly pressed on. One Frenchman fell, a second, then a third. Others lay wounded. Ammunition was starting to run low.

De Maisonneuve realized that their only hope was to retreat toward the *chemin de traîne* that lay somewhere at their backs. Unlike his men, all the Indians appeared to have snowshoes, and the French would be further hampered by having to carry away their wounded. However, wood dragged along the *chemin* had left its surface hard, "and snowshoes," Dollier records, "would be less necessary there to make any speed."

The French began an orderly retreat, pausing from time to time to slow down their pursuers with a disciplined volley. At last they found the *chemin*, which stretched back toward the stockade. With safety in sight, their discipline broke down, and most began making a run for it.

De Maisonneuve, of sterner stuff, continued to fire, covering his fleeing men with his two pistols. He soon was left behind, exposed to the fast-approaching Indians.

Suddenly, the Indians paused, not from fear but to give the honour of capturing de Maisonneuve to their chief. This man leapt forward and once more de Maisonneuve raised his pistols. The Indian ducked, just as the first trigger was pulled, but the pistol misfired. For a moment, de Maisonneuve seemed doomed, but the chief's advantage was lost as quickly as it had arisen. As he stood up to pounce, the second pistol discharged as it was meant to, killing him instantly. The rest of the Indians, rather than overwhelming de Maisonneuve, swept up the body of their dead leader and hustled it away.

Even so, de Maisonneuve's desperate bravery might have been for nothing had there not been yet another misfiring. His men, in leaving him behind on the *chemin,* went charging on toward the stockade in such disorder that one of its defenders, heedless of who might be a friend or who a foe, set his match to a cannon mounted on a bastion. Fortunately, the cannon was badly primed and it failed to fire. "Had it done so," Dollier writes, "it was laid so truly along the little road by which they approached that it would have killed them all." By such a chance did the French hang on to Ville Marie.

Dollier was a man of considerable parts. He had been a cavalry officer in France before taking holy orders as a Sulpician priest. Vigorous, physically imposing, it was said he could hold aloft a man sitting in each of his hands. He was sent to Canada by the Sulpicians in 1666 and soon was proselytizing far up-country. He accompanied a party of French explorers during a yearlong expedition in 1669-70 that demonstrated the Great Lakes were indeed connected. Shortly after his return to Montreal, he was appointed the Sulpicians' superior in Canada and seigneur of Montreal Island.

He found much to occupy him during his thirty-five years in Canada. He helped administer the Hôtel-Dieu after its founder, Jeanne Mance, died in 1673. He started building the Sulpician seminary that, more than three centuries later, is still a part of Place d'Armes. He encouraged education in the town. He strove—unsuccessfully, as it turned out—to dig the first canal bypassing the Lachine Rapids. And somewhere along the way he found the time to become Montreal's first historian.

When Dollier first arrived from France, it was clear the once-fragile community was beginning to acquire a certain substance. It was well established on the Coteau Saint-Louis, where as many as ninety-four houses stood. Small barns, storage sheds and other structures had also begun to spread from the riverfront up the slope. The settlement's population was comfortably over 700, vastly more than de Maisonneuve's original few dozen, and the newcomers were often more interested in trading with the Indians than in converting them. It's no coincidence the name of the place was beginning to change, from Ville Marie to Montreal.

Dollier was determined to organize this growth. So one morning—March 12, 1672, to be precise—an odd little party started to make its way up the Coteau Saint-Louis. In addition to Dollier, there was Bénigne Basset, who wore hats as the court clerk, as a notary and as a land surveyor. And there were others, bearing some odd-looking stones.

Dollier, Basset and the others were about to lay out a formal grid of nine streets for the little town, two long ones and, crossing more or less at right angles, seven shorter ones. Its pattern shapes Old Montreal to this day.

There already were paths and cart tracks in Ville Marie that people, willy nilly, had traced out themselves in their daily routines. At least two even had names, Saint-Paul along the river and Saint-Joseph, today's Saint-Sulpice. This latter went up the slope from Saint-Paul and down the other side to a small bridge over the muddy Ruisseau Saint-Martin. Dollier took advantage of this pattern when he could. But other streets were wholly new, and for some he had to exercise his right as seigneur to expropriate land he needed from plots that had already been granted. The actual construction of the new streets—the clearing away of brush and other obstacles, the widening where necessary—stretched out over the next several years, by which time even more streets were beginning to appear.

The most important of Dollier's new streets was laid along the spine of the Coteau Saint-Louis. Not only was this street the widest, at thirty feet, but right in the middle of it, dominating the community, the Sulpician was determined to build a new parish church.

No matter how the community's name might be changing, Dollier had no doubt about what this street—and the church that would begin

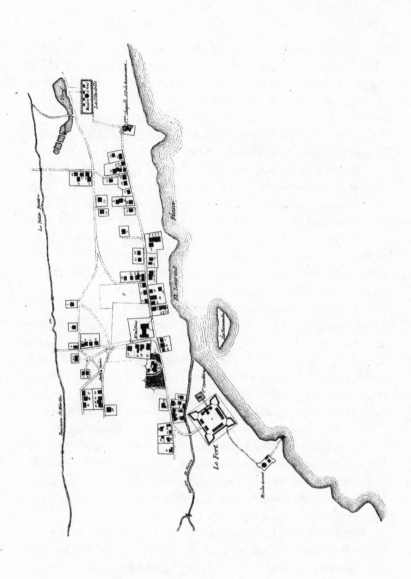

Map of Montreal 1650-72 shows Paul de Maisonneuve's fort and,
across the Rivière Saint-Pierre on the Coteau Saint-Louis,
Jeanne Mance's Hôtel-Dieu.
(From *Le Vieux Montréal* by Pierre-Louis Morin, 1884.)

to rise three months later—would be called. "We gave to this most important street the name Notre-Dame," Basset wrote later in his official report, "to remind the inhabitants of Montreal in perpetuity that this town as well as all the Island of Montreal were dedicated to Mary, patron of the country." The street also linked two structures vital to the community, a windmill where the street petered out to the east and its only public well, at the site of the new church.

The strange-looking stones that Dollier's helpers carried up the slope that March morning were survey markers, each inset with a leaden stamp bearing the arms of the seminary. Eight were set out along the line of the future Rue Notre-Dame. Others, opposite a certain window here, at the edge of a garden there, were for the other streets: Saint-Jacques, parallel to Notre-Dame, and Saint-François, Saint-Pierre, du Calvaire, Saint-Lambert, Saint-Gabriel, Saint-Charles and the already existing Saint-Joseph, lying athwart.

Not just saints but at the same time more contemporary figures are commemorated in these names. In Saint-Jacques we are invited to hear an echo of Jean-Jacques Olier, founder of the Sulpician order, while Saint-Paul recalls Montreal's pious founder, Paul de Maisonneuve. Rue Saint-Lambert was named in memory of Lambert Closse, "this brave major who died in defence of the country" fighting the Iroquois in 1662. Saint-François, later Saint-François-Xavier, was for Dollier himself.

The official report, or *procès-verbal,* drawn up by Basset four months later to describe that March day's surveying makes only two or three passing references to compass directions. Instead, the new streets, time and again, are described in relation to existing land holdings. Those plots, in turn, were oriented according to the course of the St. Lawrence River as it swept past the island.

Perhaps, in their apparent indifference to the compass, Basset and Dollier were already thinking the way Montrealers do today: no matter what the compass might say, streets like Notre-Dame run "east-west" while streets like Saint-Lambert, which has evolved into today's Boulevard Saint-Laurent, go "north-south." It made comforting sense to these early Montrealers, we can speculate, that the St. Lawrence flowed not north to the sea but east—to a sea beyond which, vastly farther to the east, lay the homes they once knew in France. These directions, for all their wonkiness, nonetheless represented a truth that was emotionally satisfying, perhaps even necessary, for settlers at the uttermost edge of European civilization.

The streets that Dollier gave to Montreal were a very early venture in urban planning in North America. The streets went where Dollier wanted them to go, and would be used the way he wanted them to be used. Notre-Dame was deliberately conceived as a spiritual axis for the community, superseding the commercial one that was developing along Saint-Paul. Crops could not be grown in the various rights-of-way, he decreed, nor animals be allowed to run unchecked, and people with property along them had to start making proper use of their holdings.

In his *procès-verbal*, Basset mentions a Place d'Armes and says it could well be renamed Place Maisonneuve to "preserve the precious memory … of the victory won on this spot by M. de Maisonneuve over the ferocious Iroquois. We are not without hope of seeing a statue to this great man raised on this spot."

But just where was this spot? As with the site of de Maisonneuve's cross on the mountain, there has been confusion over the centuries.

Almost certainly, it was not the Place d'Armes we know today, despite de Maisonneuve's magnificent bronze presence there, high atop its stone column. Rather, it was much closer to the river, approximately on the site of the present Place Royale. (Adding to the confusion, there is a second Place Royale to account for. That is the name Champlain gave to the spot where he landed in 1611 and that de Maisonneuve chose for Ville Marie thirty-one years later.)

The Place d'Armes of Basset's day was simply an open area on the riverbank. A twice-weekly market was held there, so naturally it was known as Place du Marché. But it was also a convenient place for soldiers to drill, and so was coming to be known by a second name, the one used in the *procès-verbal*. Meanwhile, up the Coteau Saint-Louis, the area where Rue Notre-Dame swung around Dollier's new church took on the name Place de la Fabrique.

The threat of Indian attack disappeared with the dawn of the eighteenth century, but not the recurring threat of fire. In June of 1721, an especially devastating blaze left half the town a charred ruin. The destruction was particularly severe near Place du Marché, and recon-

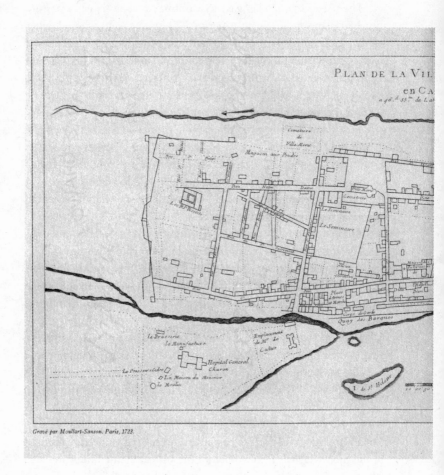

Gédéon de Catalogne's 1723 map is probably the first to show
Montreal's streets, buildings and fortifications accurately.
(Engraved by Pierre Moullart-Sanson, Paris.)

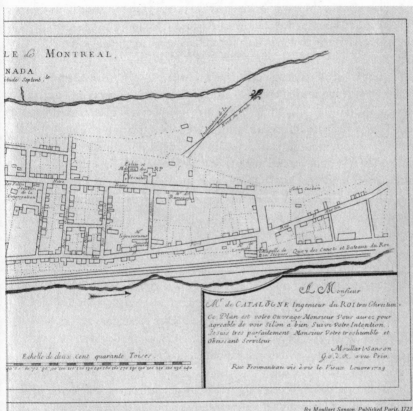

LE de MONTREAL.

NADA.

Ce Plan est votre Ouvrage Monsieur Vous aurez pour agreable de voir Silon a bien Suivre votre Intention. Je suis tres parfaitement Monsieur Votre treshumble et Obeissant Serviteur

Echelle de deux Cent quarante Toises.

By Moullart Sanson, Published Paris, 1723

struction in the area forced the soldiers to look for somewhere else to exercise. The obvious choice was Place de la Fabrique, and in moving there the soldiers displaced its old name with one that came along with them, Place d'Armes.

Place du Marché stayed behind, and so prosaic a name made it no home for de Maisonneuve's heroics. No wonder, for most people, that the supposed site of that 1644 skirmish deftly moved up the slope to the new Place d'Armes as well.

In 1716, a military engineer named Gaspard-Joseph Chaussegros de Léry was sent out from France. The following year, stone walls to his design began to rise around the townsite that Dollier had in effect laid out. They were finally finished in 1744. But while Montreal was no longer a missionary outpost, it hadn't evolved into much of a military one, either. The sprawling pattern of rampart, scarp, fosse, counterscarp and glacis was a hindrance to the town's emerging importance as a commercial centre. Time and again, new gates were punched through on the south side to give streets access to the busy port. Early in the nineteenth century, the walls were demolished.

Walls or no walls, a few of those streets going down to the port kept right on going, at least in winter. Once the river froze solid, roads were laid out across the ice to link the heart of the town with the South Shore. With the ferries laid up for the season, the ice roads were the only way across for most people—and a free one, to boot. Even the mighty Victoria Bridge couldn't make them obsolete, for only in 1899, four decades after it opened for trains, was the bridge modified to carry wagons, cars and other wheeled traffic as well.

While countless informal tracks criss-crossed each other, a few were laid out and maintained by the authorities as a public service. One of the most important of these would cross more or less in a straight line from the Old Port to Saint-Lambert. Another would bend past Île Sainte-Hélène, bound for Longueuil. As well, a little downstream, an ice road generally went straight across from the suburb of Hochelaga to Longueuil. However, the precise routes would vary slightly from year to year, depending on the nature of the ice. For example, huge frozen blocks thrown up by the pressure of ice farther upstream had to be avoided.

Small evergreens set in the snowbanks beside the route marked the way across, much as they do for snowmobilers venturing onto frozen lakes and rivers in our own day. Gangs of workmen would do their best to keep the track open and smooth, though it wasn't always easy. Strong winds might leave drifts of snow across the route. Weak spots, even holes or great fissures, might appear in the ice, making detours necessary.

All the day long, sleighs could be seen shuttling back and forth. Woodcutters brought firewood to the city. A farmer might have his produce or his wife some knitting to sell on market day. Fodder had to be brought in for the city's animals.

Other people, more intent on buying than selling, were drawn by the wide variety of things in Montreal's shops. Occasionally, a man with no sleigh of his own—or perhaps simply to break the monotony of winter—might make the two-mile trek on foot.

Of course, the ferries to the South Shore didn't stop one day and the ice roads open up the day after. During the shoulder seasons of early winter and early spring, drifting ice would make it dangerous for ferries to cross, or soft ice would make it impossible for sleighs. Only with the coming of the deep freeze would Montreal's isolation be relieved a little.

The freeze might come quite late, as an item in the *Montreal Herald* of January 21, 1815, indicates:

"On Tuesday the Ice took fast ... and roads were made in the usual directions, which already afford a vast supply of wood and Hay for this city. Fresh pork comes in abundance from the Eastern Townships. Small Hogs sell at 60s. per 100 lb. The finest cured hams sell at 1s. per lb. by the small quantity."

Travelling on the informal ice roads could be dangerous at times, for they were scarcely maintained at all. But even on the official ice roads, nightfall or a snowstorm could make even the most experienced driver lose his way. And that might spell disaster. An unseen lump of hard-packed snow could overturn a sleigh. A weak spot in the ice could give way, sending a sleigh into the frigid water and its unlucky occupants to almost certain death.

This nearly happened to an Englishman being taken by sleigh to La Prairie in 1808. His driver curved around Nuns' Island and started across as he had always done, but the morning was unusually hazy and disorienting. No shoreline, no landmarks, could be seen, no matter where the two men looked. Two hours passed and still they had not reached their destination. They were lost.

Fortunately, they met a sleigh going in the opposite direction, and from its driver realized what must have happened. The Englishman learned to his horror that instead of crossing the river they had headed up it and were now but a few hundred yards from the open water at the foot of the Lachine Rapids. Had it not been for their fortunate encounter with the other sleigh, they might have kept right on going, until it was too late.

Trouble might arise even in fine weather. One day in 1881, a wagon on runners got stuck in an unexpected hollow in one of the ice roads. Another carter stopped, unhitched his team and used it to pull the first wagon free. In the confusion, however, it collided with a passing sleigh. The sleigh was undamaged, but the unfortunate wagon went up an incline and then toppled over. Only when more men arrived on the scene and righted the wagon could it at last get under way again in earnest.

Nonetheless, for most people the winter crossings were uneventful, a familiar part of winter's routine. In fact, the ice worked so well as a natural bridge that a group of railway executives concocted an audacious idea. If it could handle a multitude of sleighs, might it also support a train?

The Victoria Bridge was owned by the Grand Trunk Railway. Other railways could use the bridge but had to pay for the privilege. Even then, they had to keep to schedules that didn't conflict with the Grand Trunk's. However, at least for a few months of the year, the ice might provide an alternative. A consortium led by the provincially owned Quebec, Montreal, Ottawa & Occidental Railway decided to try.

In January 1880, temporary tracks were laid parallel to the ice road between Hochelaga and Longueuil, and soon all was ready. It was a Saturday morning, the last day of the month. Crowds of Montrealers pressed down to the Hochelaga terminal, where a small locomotive was busily building up steam. A fir tree was festively mounted on the engine's cowcatcher, and two open cars in which passengers could stand were coupled behind.

Sleighs shuttle back and forth across the frozen St. Lawrence, c. 1915.
(Photo by S.J. Hayward.)

Evergreens stuck in the snow marked the ice roads, and drivers who
strayed risked disaster.
(From *L'Opinion Publique*, April 23, 1870.)

A montage titled "Sketches on the Ice Railroad, a Locomotive
Gone Astray" shows the view toward Longueuil, "great excitement
amongst the natives," a map of the ice railroad's route, the accident,
the view toward Hochelaga, and men measuring the thickness of the ice.
(Illustration from the *Canadian Illustrated News*, January 15, 1881.)

A series of engravings in the *Canadian Illustrated News* preserves the remarkable day: late-arriving passengers scrambling on board, a long line of sleighs racing to keep up with the train once it got under way, a pause in the middle of the river so a Notman photographer could record the scene, a champagne reception for everyone at the Longueuil end. The crossing went off without a hitch, and for the rest of the winter the ice railroad provided another way to get people and goods across the river.

The following winter, the service began earlier, on January 5, and promised to be just as successful. Alas, it was not to be. On that first day, a line of cars was pulled across the river by horses to test the strength of the ice, and all seemed well. But when a locomotive tried to repeat the crossing, the ice began to give way. The heavy locomotive tipped onto its side and crashed through. The crew just barely managed to leap clear.

Nothing daunted, the railway immediately laid new tracks to swing around the hole in the ice, and the service resumed with a new locomotive two days later. But it was an ill omen. While there were no more serious interruptions that winter, the mishap was a pointed reminder of Nature's whims. When winter the following year proved unusually mild, the service was late in starting and could be maintained only sporadically.

Cold weather returned for the winter of 1883, when management of the ice railroad fell to the other consortium member, the South Eastern Railway. But the South Eastern was already in financial trouble and was soon absorbed by the Canadian Pacific. The new owners had no interest in such frivolities. It proved to be the ice railroad's last year.

The ice roads were a kind of extension of Montreal's streetscape onto the river. But sometimes, especially in early spring, it worked the other way round: the river extended itself into the streets. Flooding might not threaten the entire community with destruction as it did with de Maisonneuve's Ville Marie, for of course suburbs well away from the waterfront were being opened up and occupied all the time. But for those who lived in the low-lying, old part of town or who did business there, the risk of high water remained a grim fact of life.

Montreal, lying just below the confluence of the Ottawa River with the St. Lawrence, is particularly exposed to snowmelt in the spring. Ice dams are another danger, especially when combined with a sudden thaw and heavy runoff. Water building up behind an ice dam can rapidly overflow riverbanks upstream. Or, when a dam suddenly disintegrates, the water allowed to surge through might attack the land immediately downstream.

A freelance reporter working for *The Gazette* in 1861 found out just how sudden this could be. On the evening of April 14, a Sunday, he was standing in Place Royale, keeping an eye on the vast blocks of ice, fifty feet high and more, that had built up in the harbour in front of him. He was waiting for the famous annual ice shove, when the ice would suddenly break loose and begin its rush downstream.

Suddenly, the ice shifted. But instead of continuing to move, it settled into a dam that the current could not get through. The waters of the St. Lawrence immediately began to back up, and the reporter was in trouble.

"The ice did shove," *The Gazette* reported, "and the water rose like a wall, suddenly, instantly. It rushed towards the spot where he was standing; he turned and ran with all his strength to escape it; but it came too swiftly for him; he had to wade through 44 inches of water before he reached the foot of St. François Xavier Street, a distance of not more than fifty yards!"

Within hours, the streets from Bonsecours Market west past Victoria Square to the foot of Mountain Street were inundated. The flood backed up from Victoria Square along Craig Street, today's Saint-Antoine but once the course of the Ruisseau Saint-Martin that Dollier de Casson knew. As much as six feet of water lay in the manufacturing and warehouse district near the entrance to the Lachine Canal.

That Sunday evening, worshipers at St. Stephen's Anglican Church in Griffintown and at the nearby Wesleyan church were among the first to be trapped. Most clambered up onto pews and chairs, too frightened to venture out. Only a handful of men in the congregations felt strong enough to brave the flooded streets and try for home, their children on their shoulders.

The sturdy Jacob Ellegood, the rector of St. Stephen's, also decided to try. He would make for the home of Montreal's mayor, Charles-Séraphin Rodier, and alert him to the growing danger. He struck out through the frigid water, which occasionally came up to his neck. Chunks of ice

The inundation of McGill Street, from the corner of Rues des Récollets,
April 15, 1861.
(The Illustrated London News, May 11, 1861.)

The spring break-up in the harbour in front of Bonsecours Market, c. 1880.
(Photo attributed to J.G. Parks, Archives nationales du Québec.)

bumped into him, scraping his already savaged skin. When he got to dry land, he began running, not just out of urgency but also to warm up.

When he arrived at Rodier's house, the mayor had to be roused from his bed. Ellegood appealed for boats to rescue his parishioners. Then he began running again, this time for his own home where he eventually sank into a hot bath.

More than the marooned Anglicans needed rescuing, of course. As Monday dawned, thousands of people were trapped in their houses, often upstairs—if indeed their houses had an upstairs to which they could retreat. Food was quickly ruined by the floodwaters and stoves were extinguished. ·

A thawed-out Ellegood was among those who were scrambling to find boats that morning. They poled or paddled along streets where, just a day before, people had walked and wagons rolled. They conveyed people to safety as best they could or, for those who wouldn't leave their homes, they left off food.

Animals suffered as well, and of course the number of animals in the city in those days, and their variety, were far different from what we know today. Some could be taken to higher ground by their owners, but time and again horses, cattle and pigs could be seen thrashing about on their own, not knowing which way to turn. A cow managed to reach a second-storey gallery on Chaboillez Square and was seen calmly feeding on something. Other creatures were less fortunate, and drowned.

Remarkably, very few people seem to have shared that fate, but this was small comfort to the family of one William Carmody. By Tuesday, the waters had begun to recede. Carmody and four others were in a canoe in the Lachine Canal, trying to lead their cows to safety. Then, near the Redpath sugar refinery, the canoe capsized and Carmody, his nineteen-year-old daughter and a young man named Ryan were drowned.

"The bodies were recovered by means of drags ... and conveyed to their homes by the Water Police," says a newspaper report. "The scene at Carmody's on Farm street, a little south of the Wellington Bridge, was very distressing when he and his daughter were brought in on boats. A number of the neighbours and his poor wife and daughters were present and gave vent to their feelings in an affecting manner."

Haphazard clearing of ice and snow did little to improve
city streets for pedestrians.
(*Canadian Illustrated News*, March 18, 1871.)

Snow removal, as seen here in Notre Dame Street c. 1880, was laborious without mechanized equipment. (Photo by Notman Studio, Montreal.)

And so it seemed to go, year after year. Amid the recurring misery, some people tried to make the best of things. The flood of 1886 was positively Noachian, the worst that Montreal had yet seen, but even at its height there was still time for frivolity. "Last night, the inhabitants of Griffintown had a good time of it," one newspaper said. "Surprise parties were formed, and jaunting about in rafts were noticed numbers of young girls who were singing and playing concertinas. The utmost good humour prevailed, and all seemed to enjoy the situation."

Other Montrealers enjoyed that year's flood in a different way. The entrepreneurial spirit being what it is, some set themselves up as instant marina operators, demanding as much as ten dollars to hire their canoes or rowboats for just half an hour. Others became ferrymen, charging what the traffic would bear to carry pedestrians over deep stretches of water.

A climax of sorts came after yet another severe flood the following year. Work to complete the massive revetment walls along the harbour-front was finally taken in hand. Unlike Chaussegros de Léry's fortifications, these were walls—dikes, in fact—that genuinely meant something to the city. The St. Lawrence might still overflow its banks occasionally and turn a few streets into canals, but never again on the scale that Montreal had known to that time.

In the spring of 1888, there was indeed ice in the streets once again, but the circumstances, while unpleasant, were much less dire. In fact, compared with what Montreal had come through the previous several years, they were almost comical.

In early April, thanks to the longer days and warmer temperatures, the snow underfoot was no longer packed down hard. Larger patches of water lay on the ground behind banks of snow and ice that hadn't been cleared away. Wheeled wagons and carriages starting to reappear from their winter hibernation were chewing up exposed stretches of roadway where the frost was coming out of the ground.

The footing was treacherous, for man and beast alike. A few streets were well nigh impassable. Shops and other businesses were noticeably less crowded as people started staying at home rather than risk a dunking in a puddle or a twisted ankle.

City council, which ordinarily preferred to let the sun take care of the snow and ice in its own good time, was growing concerned. This year, the melt was exposing an unusual amount of animal droppings and other waste. The stench was growing. So was the possibility of disease.

At least one city clergyman found inspiration in the fetid mess for his sermon that Sunday. From the pulpit of St. Bartholomew's Church, Bishop Brandram Ussher thundered on a text from the Song of Solomon: "I will rise now, and go about the city in the streets, and in the broad ways." Thus he set his theme, and soon his rhetoric had glided smoothly from deploring filth in the streets to filth of the moral variety.

The following day, city council finally decided to hire a few casual labourers to start a serious cleanup of the streets. But by then a group of about 200 citizens had taken matters into their own hands. Some were quite prominent. They included two former mayors, Henry Starnes and James McShane. There were prominent businessmen like publisher John Lovell and Henry Hogan, owner of the city's best hotel. Member of Parliament J.J. Curran turned out, as well as several lawyers and at least seven local militia officers.

They assembled with picks, shovels and other tools around two o'clock that afternoon. They had also laid on several dozen wagons. Led by "a gentleman performing on a bugle," they descended on St. James Street. There they set to work, and soon pile after pile of the ice beside the roadway had been broken up. The wagons began hauling away filth and ice, leaving at least one stretch of the street quite clear.

For some of the men, more used to comfortable homes and offices, the demands of physical labour were daunting. According to one report, some of them marched purposefully with their tools toward McGill Street where they made a pretence of working, "but the exercise was evidently too violent for the amateur navvies, for they quickly dropped it."

But the street was one of the most prestigious in the city, and however effective their actual work the amateur navvies were certainly making their point. City council met again that evening, and while several councillors grumbled, dismissing "the shovel brigade as a pack of schoolboys" who made the city look bad, most praised the stunt. The city surveyor was ordered to hire another 100 proper workmen and set them to work the following day.

The citizen cleaners were not totally convinced that council was in earnest. They showed up as well, to do a little work on their own but really to see if the city would genuinely follow through on its resolve of the previous night. Indeed, some wits began to wonder what would happen when the two gangs, one in top hats and the other in tuques and cloth caps, met up. But as it happened, not much. The top hats, finally satisfied that they had won through, did what the penny-pinchers on council generally hoped the snow would do on its own. They simply melted away.

The concern that filth in the streets might lead to an outbreak of disease was natural enough, for the memory of what happened to Montreal three years before still ached. In 1885, a devastating smallpox epidemic struck the city. Some 3,200 people died, plus an unknown number in the outlying suburbs.

At the height of the smallpox, a walking tour as unusual as the city has ever seen was organized. It made its way not through the streets of Montreal but under them.

The epidemic was particularly virulent in the densely packed neighbourhoods east of the downtown core. Was blocked-up sewage contributing to the contagion? Would a vigorous flushing of the city's sewers help?

The city engineer, P.W. St. George, didn't think so. The main sewers were not especially old—scarcely more than a couple of decades in most cases—and so far as he was concerned, the normal flow through them was already perfectly adequate for the job. Arranging for a special cleaning and flushing, he said, would achieve nothing for the city but added expense.

Yet still the suspicion that there was something wrong with the sewers would not die. His words having failed to silence the doubters, an exasperated St. George decided to act.

On the morning of September 7, a curious party assembled at the corner of Sherbrooke and Victoria streets, across from McGill University. A manhole in the pavement lay open. Gathered around it, in addition to St. George, were three other city officials and, most important, a pair of reporters from the *Montreal Star* and *The Gazette*. Each man put on an oilskin slicker and high-topped rubber boots. Each was given a lamp and a stout wooden stick with an iron ferrule. Finally, St. George handed cheroots all round.

At the engineer's signal, one of the city employees walked on ahead down Victoria Street, a ladder on his shoulder. The rest of the party, St. George going first, descended through the manhole. Fifteen feet below lay a world that few Montrealers had ever seen. St. George was gambling that, thanks to some timely newspaper coverage, many might at least come to understand it.

The five men found themselves standing in a brick-lined tunnel about six feet high and four feet across, with a noticeable flow of foul liquid perhaps six inches deep passing over their feet. St. George urged his companions to puff on their cheroots as if their lives depended on it. He was being droll, for the cigar smoke could only mask the stink of the vapours, not eliminate them. In any event, the air was not as bad as the reporters feared. This was because St. George had ordered manholes along their route to be opened in advance. (What householders and shopkeepers along the route thought about the resulting change in their air quality is not recorded.)

The subterranean tourists set off along the line of Victoria Street but soon turned left. Their route would follow an elaborate, three-and-a-half-mile zigzag toward Rue Monarque, near the Molson brewery and the St. Lawrence. Often, they could see smaller municipal sewers feeding in from one side or the other. After a time, St. George told them they had moved beneath Ontario Street and were following it east toward Amherst. Then it was a turn to Ste. Catherine, east again to Papineau and finally down once more toward the river.

They had to be careful of their footing, of course, and occasionally were forced to bend nearly double to get past low spots in the tunnels' construction. Yet, thanks to the open manholes every 200 yards or so, the gloom wasn't especially Stygian. At the manholes, the city employee keeping pace checked to be sure they were all right. Perhaps the reporters were reassured that his ladder was ready to help with a fast exit, should an accident befall anyone. Or perhaps they were made nervous by the ladder, an ominous sign that St. George thought an accident was possible. We do not know.

The first sewer, under Victoria Street, had been built in 1870. But even the older ones, dating back to 1863, proved to be in good shape. They were stained, and sediment occasionally oozed through cracks in the masonry. Otherwise, *The Gazette* later reported, they "were as fresh and as sound as when first constructed." Most important, there was no sign in them of dammed-up sewage: "The velocity of the current which carries off the sewage is about five feet per 1.5 second, and ... if all the hydrants in the city were turned on at once they would have but very little effect when compared with the natural current."

Nonetheless, there was fault to be found. Every once in a while, St. George pointed out small drains constructed not of brick but of wood. They were connections to the municipal sewers from houses and other private buildings, and in most cases they were old and rotting, partly clogged with what the *Star* delicately called "offensive matter." A restricted flow through them would be better than no flow at all, which was the reality of the outdoor privies that countless Montrealers still depended on, but that was small comfort to St. George.

City ordinances banned wooden drains in new construction, but the older ones were allowed to moulder on. The city engineer had been

Place d'Armes was once unadorned and wide open to carriages.
(Drawing by John Murray, engraved by Bourne, Montreal c. 1850.)

pressing council to step in, replace the private drains with proper piping and bill the property owners accordingly, but so far he had been rebuffed.

Stumbling and splashing about, the five men finally reached their destination, an open manhole in Rue Monarque. It was three-and-a-half hours after they had set out. One after another, they scaled the ladder and stepped onto the street, "glad indeed to again breathe once more the pure air of heaven."

Keeping the streets clean was one thing; giving them something more, a certain aesthetic cachet, was another. Statues in the streets and squares of Montreal, especially of lay figures, weren't nearly as numerous in the late nineteenth century as they are today. Nelson's Monument in Place Jacques-Cartier and Queen Victoria's statue in the square bearing her name were rare exceptions. A bust of King George III had briefly graced Place d'Armes. But it had disappeared long ago, and now there was nothing there save a rather elegant fountain.

Late in the 1870s, a group of prominent Montrealers decided that proper statuary should be returned to Place d'Armes. The 250th anniversary of the city's birth was little more than a decade away. What could be more fitting than a memorial—and something heroic, not a mere bust—to the city's founder? What better site than the heart of the old town, the square in front of Notre Dame Church? Thus might Bénigne Basset's fond hope "of seeing a statue to this great man raised" finally come true.

Napoléon Bourassa, a much-acclaimed artist, sketched a design for a monument, and his pupil Louis-Philippe Hébert rendered a model from it. Sad to say, it was all rather banal. De Maisonneuve stood flat-footed atop a tall column. Though wearing armour, he looked meek and priest-like with his right arm raised in blessing. The precariously perched beavers spouting water at his feet did nothing to enhance his dignity. The fund-raising committee disbanded, and enthusiasm for the project quickly began to fade.

But it didn't die entirely. In 1882, Abbé Hospice-Anthelme Verreau, a well-known educator and antiquarian, took up the cause, and by the time the decade was drawing to a close the flames had been fanned back into life. As one historically minded Montrealer, F.W. Henshaw, declared in 1890, a statue should be erected as "nearly as possible on the very spot upon which (de Maisonneuve) built his fort and spent his first night in what is now Montreal. Custom House square should be honoured as the site." The idea had some merit, though once again the history was dubious, for Custom House Square—that is, Place Royale—was not Pointe à Callières.

Place d'Armes remained the preferred site, even though it was too late to meet a deadline of May 1892. Unfazed, city council commissioned Hébert to create a suitable monument on his own. By then, he was no longer a promising though inexperienced apprentice in Bourassa's atelier. His commissions already included imposing statues of various soldiers and politicians, including Charles de Salaberry in Châteauguay and Sir George Étienne Cartier in Ottawa. He had been working in the artistic milieu of Paris for several years. Though scarcely forty years old, he had emerged as the Canadian sculptor *sans pareil*.

The cornerstone for the pedestal was laid in Place d'Armes in the anniversary year, but that was all. Yet when Hébert's model for the statue itself finally arrived from France the following September, it was clear that the wait was worthwhile. This de Maisonneuve seemed almost alive, far more dynamic than what the sculptor had produced with Bourassa fourteen years before. This time it was possible to see, in his solemn yet exulting face, a true soldier of God. "Maisonneuve was very religious," Hébert explained, "so I have made the face that of a soldier and monk combined."

The finished, full-sized bronze was delivered in time for a gala unveiling on Dominion Day, 1895. The day itself threatened rain, prompting one newspaper to comment archly on the "flutter in the minds of numerous belles" that their pretty dresses might be ruined. But there were compensations: "When one considers the opportunities it afforded for cosy flirtations under cover of friendly umbrellas, and for numerous acts of self-denial on the part of devoted swains, probably the rain added zest to the day."

As it turned out, the showers held off during the morning's ceremonies. Dozens of city councillors, military figures, judges and leading members of various other professions, many with their wives, filled the dignitaries' enclosure. There also were almost as many clergymen, including several from the Protestant denominations. Beyond the enclosure, the square itself was thronged with less favoured but equally animated spectators.

Promptly at ten a.m., Lieutenant-Governor Joseph-Adolphe Chapleau and his suite arrived, and the speeches began. Judge Siméon Pagnuelo, the committee chairman, sang de Maisonneuve's praises and then invited Chapleau to handle the actual unveiling. This he did, to loud applause—but not loud enough to prevent a few people over-hearing the veteran politician say it was the best piece of string-pulling he'd ever managed to accomplish.

Chapleau also read a speech on behalf of the governor general, Lord Aberdeen, who was unable to attend. Aberdeen recalled that de Maisonneuve, after shabby treatment by the governor of New France, was recalled to the mother country in 1665 and never saw Montreal again: "I may be permitted, therefore, as the successor of that governor, to offer to the illustrious founder of Montreal the tardy recompense of regretting the wrongs he suffered, and to offer today my solemn homage to his virtues and to his memory."

It was a gracious touch. Less gracious, at least in modern ears, was the condescending, Eurocentric way that various speakers referred to the Indians and their deadly attacks on Ville Marie. De Maisonneuve and his companions arrived "for the sole purpose of bringing to poor, miserable, wretched, heathen Indians the light and comfort of Christian civilization," Judge Pagnuelo said. The settlers found a land "as yet undisturbed save … perhaps by the whiz of the red man's arrow speeding on its mission of death," said former mayor William Hingston.

Several speakers, Hingston among them, confirmed that Hébert's magnificent statue stood on the very spot where de Maisonneuve "alone … encountered the savage, and where in self-defence he slew him." Yet no one in the crowd that Dominion Day was of a mind to object that the Indians were merely defending their land, or that de Maisonneuve's famous exploit occurred elsewhere. That would be for another time.

When the ceremonies finally concluded, Abbé Louis-Frédéric Colin, the Sulpicians' superior, invited the lieutenant-governor, his wife and several other ladies and gentlemen to take a light lunch in the gardens of the seminary adjoining Notre Dame Church. It was the same seminary whose construction had been initiated by Abbé Colin's long-ago predecessor François Dollier de Casson.

"It was a rich treat for all those who visited this beautiful retreat," The Gazette said. "For the first time in two hundred years, ladies entered these precincts."

Chapter Two

~

A cat may look on a king.

–John Heywood, "Proverbs," 1546

We've had kings and princes among us. One of them most assuredly was not Eleazer Williams.

Did Williams deliberately set out to fool everyone, or was he simply fooling himself? It's impossible to say. But sometime around 1840 he got it into his head that he was the son of the guillotined Louis XVI and Marie Antoinette. He was the so-called Lost Dauphin, he claimed, and rightfully King Louis XVII of France. Not bad for someone who had been born not at Versailles in 1785, but several years later in a rough bower on the shores of Lake George, in upstate New York.

To be sure, Williams's pedigree was remarkable enough. Through his father, a prominent Mohawk from Kahnawake, he was descended from the Puritan divine John Williams. In 1704, this Williams and his family were among the captives taken during the infamous Mohawk raid on Deerfield, Massachusetts. Some of the captives were adopted into Mohawk families. One of them was Williams's seven-year-old daughter Eunice, Eleazer's great-grandmother.

One day as a child, Eleazer dove into Lake George and struck his head. The accident was serious enough that from then on he bore the Mohawk name Onwarenhiiaki, "his head is split" or "divided air" being among several interpretations. Perhaps his royal delusions were rooted here. Or perhaps they can be traced to a meeting in 1806 with a priest in Boston who suggested the young Eleazer appeared to have French blood in him.

Though baptized as a Roman Catholic, Eleazer was educated in a Protestant school in Longmeadow, Massachusetts. In time he became an itinerant missionary, first for the Congregationalists and then the Episcopalians, striving to win his fellow natives away from Rome. He did reasonably well for a time in Wisconsin, where he persuaded some Oneidas to settle, but his growing vanity and other signs of instability led to his downfall there. He returned to the more familiar ground of Akwesasne, near Cornwall, Ontario, and Kahnawake, across the river from Montreal, but had precious little success there, either.

Williams probably began dropping hints about his supposed royal lineage sometime after his return to Canada from Wisconsin. Certainly from about 1840 on, there were rumours aplenty, which he was happy to encourage.

In truth, the doomed dauphin of France had wasted away under the wretched conditions of the Temple prison in Paris. He died on June 8, 1795—but not according to Eleazer Williams. His story went like this.

After his father's execution in January 1793 and his mother's nine months later, he—ahem, the young Louis—indeed remained locked up in the Temple. His cruel jailer, a one-time cobbler named Antoine Simon, frequently beat him, leaving his face and body scarred. Then came a miracle. Royalists managed to bribe his captors and spirit the boy away. But he could not be seen in public, not yet. Being the throne's rightful heir made him a threat to the revolution. His life was in profound danger, and a haven across the Atlantic was not too far away.

Later that same year, a mysterious French couple named De Jardin showed up in Albany, New York. They had a boy with them named Louis; he was scarred and in poor health. Several days later, the De Jardins disappeared, leaving the boy in the hands of royalist sympathizers. Eventually, he was adopted by the Williams family of Kahnawake. No wonder no proper baptismal certificate for Eleazer could ever be found.

The story, fantastic though it was, began moving from whispered rumour to the pages of U.S. and French periodicals as early as 1849. But it really took off in 1853 with the publication of an article titled "Have We a Bourbon Among Us?" in *Putnam's Magazine*. The author, John H. Hanson, followed it up a year later with a book almost 500 pages long titled *The Lost Dauphin*.

It made for sensational reading, and for a time Williams was lionized. He gave lectures. He was introduced to famous people. He sat for portraits (and the artists weren't above heightening the supposed Bourbon likeness).

But it wasn't to last. Spoilsports soon began to pick the story apart. Even Williams's elderly mother scorned his pretensions. The absence of a baptismal certificate? That was because she had borne him in the bush while off on a hunting foray, far from any church. The scars? They were from the cuts he constantly picked up as a boy from stones and thorns, made worse by the scrofula to which many in the Williams family were prey—to say nothing of his own deliberate scratching at the wounds.

If Williams was who he claimed to be, the carping was undoubted *lèse-majesté,* a clear insult to royal dignity. But he wasn't majestic to begin with, and we hadn't had a Bourbon among us after all. Eleazer Williams died, discredited and in poverty, at Akwesasne in 1858.

However, Montreal had already seen genuine royalty several generations before. It first came in the person of Prince William Henry, the third son of King George III. The prince was serving in the Royal Navy, and in July 1786 sailed from Britain in command of the twenty-eight-gun frigate *Pegasus.* He was bound for the West Indies, but during his fifteen months in North American waters he was in Quebec City at least twice and Montreal once. During his week-long stay in Montreal, in September 1787, the future King William IV visited the Sulpician seminary and was feted at a dinner given by the local Masonic lodge.

About that time, plans were afoot to establish a university for the colony in Quebec City. Largely outside the orbit of the Catholic Church, it would offer a secular education and accept English and French students alike. Despite the secular bias, there was support for the idea in some church quarters, and soon the Sulpicians were pressing for an affiliate in Montreal.

Guy Carleton, the governor-in-chief who had been created Baron Dorchester in 1786, was keen on the proposed institution. However, he balked when it was proposed to call the Montreal branch Collège Dorchester. The Sulpicians then thought of their recent royal visitor. Like Carleton, the prince had also acquired a new title as the Duke of Clarence, so a possible Collège Clarence at least had events of the day to recommend it.

In September 1787, the Duke of Clarence, the future
King William IV, visited Montreal.
(Portrait by Abraham Wivell, 1825.)

Nonetheless, the prince had no discernible interest in the life of the mind. He was far more interested in womanizing, drinking, cards, and his naval career, in that order, so perhaps it's not entirely a bad thing that the college project eventually fizzled out. Montreal was deprived of secular higher education for at least another generation, though the affair did have the virtue of sparing the city a name that would have been something of a joke. (For his part, of course, the long-dead Dorchester had no say in the matter when a Carleton College did emerge, albeit in Ottawa, in 1942. It became Carleton University in 1957.)

It's hard to imagine Prince William ever being aware that his new name had been spurned. Yet he could hardly avoid another piece of *lèse-majesté* that had been right under his nose during his Montreal visit. But first, the background:

The Sulpician seminary where he dined in 1787 stands to this day on Place d'Armes. In 1766, six years after Montreal fell to the British, another of the many fires that have been the bane of Montreal's history devastated the core of the town. In faraway London, a wealthy philanthropist named Jonas Hanway organized a relief campaign in aid of this new outpost of the empire. Within months, £8,500, two fire pumps and, of all things, a marble bust of King George III arrived.

King George himself contributed the bust. It was the work of Joseph Wilton, soon to be a founding member of the Royal Academy, and was probably the first to be executed of the king after his ascension to the throne in 1760.

Several years were to pass, however, before it would be revealed to public view in Montreal. The bust had to be displayed properly, and to this end it would rest on a pedestal in the middle of Place d'Armes, sheltered from the elements by a kind of canopy above. Hanway, said to have been the first Englishman to walk the streets of the capital carrying an umbrella, would have understood.

This confection was unveiled on October 7, 1773, and a prominent Montrealer named Luc de La Corne decided that the town's church bells should be rung in celebration. Luc de La Corne had been a French soldier of distinction before the conquest, and he never entirely reconciled himself to the new British regime. But he was also a realist. There could be no harm in the occasional, well-chosen profession of loyalty.

La Corne went to the commander of the British troops in Montreal and urged that the bells be rung. This officer had no particular objection, but he also had no wish to annoy the ecclesiastical authorities needlessly. It was not for him to give such an order, he replied, but rather for Étienne Montgolfier, the superior of the Sulpicians, to do so.

Abbé Montgolfier made it a general point not to attend such ceremonies, and had not been invited to this one. He would stay put in the seminary, and there the ardent La Corne hastened to present himself. He pressed Montgolfier not once, not twice, but three times about the bells. Finally the exasperated priest replied: "The bells are an instrument of religion, and have never served in military or civil ceremonies. ... If the military commander wants the bells to be rung, let him give the order to the beadle himself. I have nothing else to say."

Back went La Corne to the British commandant, who by then was also growing weary of the importunate Canadian. The result of the day's buck-passing was that the king's marble image was presented to the city a little less enthusiastically than even casual royalists might have wished. The bells never did ring.

About this time, the ferment that was erupting in the American Revolution could be felt in Montreal, at least among a few of its citizens. On May 1, 1775, not two years after the bust's unveiling, the city awoke to find that it had been vandalized. It was blackened with tar, and something resembling a bishop's mitre was jammed on its head. A rosary of potatoes was strung about its neck, together with a cross on which could be read *Voilà le Pape du Canada et le Sot Anglois.*

Everybody was outraged, though for different reasons. The military authorities blamed the merchants, seeing nothing but traitorous republicans among them. French-speaking Catholics blamed the Protestants for insulting the pope. English-speaking Protestants blamed the Catholics for demeaning the king. Some said it was the work of the Jews. When a certain Sieur Le Pailleur upbraided Ezekiel Solomons, a Jewish fur trader, they started pummelling one another. Le Pailleur was knocked to the ground and for a brief time Solomons was arrested.

Governor Carleton offered a reward of $200 to anyone identifying the perpetrators, with a pardon on offer should the informant be an accomplice. The merchants added 100 *louis* they raised among themselves. But nothing happened; lips remained sealed. The bust was more or less cleaned up and resumed its watch over the square.

The next day, a drummer, a crier and several British officers strode into the square. When a drum roll had got everyone's attention, the crier announced that the officers were adding fifty guineas to the reward. One of those listening was former François-Marie Picoté de Belestre. He had served with distinction under the former French regime, and even more than La Corne had made his peace with the new British order. The vandals, he growled, should be whipped by the hangman and then banished from the colony; no, better still, "they deserved to be hanged."

This was too much for a young man of republican sympathies named David Franks. "Hanged! What, for such a trifle?" This infuriated Picoté. "You are a giddy-headed, insolent spark!" he exclaimed, then accused Franks of knowing more about the vandalism than he was letting on. The two men began shoving each other, and when Picoté grabbed the younger man's nose and twisted it, Franks started throwing punches. The fight "deprived the old gentleman of his senses for some time and was the occasion of some loss of blood." Onlookers had to pull Franks away.

The magistrates took a dim view of Franks's part in the dust-up. "Every good subject ought to look upon the said insult to His Majesty's bust as an act of the most atrocious nature," they intoned, "and as deserving of the utmost abhorrence. ... Therefore all declarations made in conversation that tend to affirm it to be a small offence ought to be esteemed criminal."

On May 4, Franks was arrested by a detachment of soldiers who, with fixed bayonets, marched him to the jail. Defiantly, however, he refused to post bail, even though he had the resources to do so. Staying behind bars, he maintained, would reveal the authorities for the royalist tyrants they truly were. Governor Carleton knew a no-win situation when he saw one. Not wishing to create a martyr, he ordered Franks's release. Even then, the young man wouldn't back down; he had to be forcibly thrown back into the street.

Late that autumn, with the American struggle for independence under way in earnest, a column of the Continental Army moved north and occupied the city, seeking to persuade Montrealers to join in the revolutionary adventure. By the following spring, however, with the Royal Navy once again able to move up the St. Lawrence, the Americans were gone. So, too, was the bust of the king.

No one knew precisely what had happened to it, though the departed invaders were the obvious culprits. The decapitated pedestal and its canopy, now sheltering nothing, looked more and more forlorn as the years passed. It was a metaphor for the fragility of monarchy on this side of the Atlantic, and Prince William could hardly have avoided the implicit mockery when he came calling on the Sulpicians in 1787. What the priests might have offered by way of explanation or even apology for this affront to his father is not known.

Canada didn't have to wait long for its next royal visitor. He was Prince William's younger brother, Edward Augustus. He had chosen a career in the army, not the navy, and he landed with his regiment, the 7th Royal Fusiliers, at Quebec City in August 1791.

The twenty-four-year-old Prince Edward was accompanied by Thérèse-Bernardine Montgenet, known as Madame de Saint-Laurent or simply Julie. They had been together since the previous November and would remain devoted to one another even when, in 1818, Edward was finally obliged to forsake her and marry legitimately, becoming soon after the father of the future Queen Victoria.

Edward's Quebec posting lasted two-and-a-half years, and during it he and Julie passed back and forth through Montreal at least once. That was in the summer of 1792. On August 11 the couple left Quebec City, bound for Newark in Upper Canada where John Graves Simcoe would be their host. Simcoe had just been appointed the new colony's first lieutenant-governor and the little settlement, today's Niagara-on-the-Lake, was his temporary capital.

Edward and Julie travelled up the St. Lawrence by carriage, by bateau, even on a barge fitted up as elegantly as could be managed with bunks and a small dining saloon. At Kingston, they would transfer to an armed schooner for the final run to the top of Lake Ontario.

Since his arrival in Canada, Edward had become friendly with the crusty James Cuthbert, despite a difference of nearly half a century in their ages. Now seventy-three, Cuthbert was the seigneur of a vast estate at Berthier, a little downstream from Montreal, so it was natural for Edward to break his journey there. As the royal party drew close, five companies of militia could be seen drawn up. They greeted the prince with cheers of *Vive le Roi! Vive la Reine! Vive son altesse le Prince Édouard!* The bells of the seigneury's chapel peeled constantly and "a salute of twenty-one small cannon was fired" as the militiamen then escorted the prince and Julie to Cuthbert's manor house. A dinner was served, and it was four o'clock that afternoon before they were on their way again. "His Royal Highness's condescending affability charmed all beholders," *The Gazette* reported.

His progress up the river caught Montrealers flat-footed. The royal party seems to have slipped right past Montreal with scarcely a nod. It was only on the prince's return from Niagara, on September 1, that "a number of the most respectable citizens of Montreal," mostly English-speaking, had organized themselves sufficiently to offer him a formal address of welcome.

Had they deliberately set out to snub him in late August? Certainly, the words they eventually got around to composing were nothing if not fulsome. The hearts of the citizenry were "replete with joy on seeing ... another of the Sons of their beloved sovereign" among them. "We are strongly impressed with a lively sense of the liberal Constitution of Government which it hath pleased his Majesty to extend to this province," it continued, "and when we behold his Son bred to the profession of Arms, for the purpose of protecting his faithful Subjects, our tribute of gratitude is the more forcibly called forth." And on, and on.

Yet there surely was a lot of blather here. For the English-speaking merchant class, the Constitution Act passed at Westminster the year before was a two-edged sword. Having a brand-new elected assembly in Lower Canada was all very well. But with its inaugural election three months earlier, the realization was fast sinking in that there were going to be more French-speaking members than English. Perhaps pique, and not some failure by Edward's staff to alert the city, explains the city's tardiness in greeting him.

In replying to the address, the prince dutifully noted the Montrealers' profession of pleasure—however strained it might have been—with the new constitution. "I shall not fail in informing His

Majesty of the very loyal and faithful attachment you so warmly express towards him," he said.

This, too, was blather. The king was famously scornful of Edward and did his best to keep him as far away as possible, preferably out of Britain entirely. If the prince ever did deign to "assure your Royal Father, the best of Sovereigns," of the loyalty of Montreal, he surely did not bother to do so in person.

Indeed, given the hostility between father and son, it's delicious to speculate that Edward might have been more amused than offended by the king's missing bust in Place d'Armes. Yet it was not to be. Two years before, the useless masonry that had accommodated the bust was declared a public nuisance and torn down. Only in 1834, when workmen were cleaning out the fifty-foot well that stood in the square, was the bust rediscovered, mud-covered but more or less in good shape otherwise. It's now in the McCord Museum on Sherbrooke Street.

Montreal's first genuine royal tour, in the sense that we now understand the term, came with the arrival of Albert Edward, the Prince of Wales, in 1860. Little more than half a century had passed, but the outpouring of civic giddiness he sparked was light-years beyond the receptions that Montreal had given the two earlier princes. This would be the real McCoy, a genuine affair of state.

Montreal was brimming with confidence in 1860. The port was booming with the revolution of steam navigation. The Grand Trunk Railway had been driven west to Toronto and Windsor and southeast to tidewater at Portland, Maine. And, most astonishing of all, the Victoria Bridge, the engineering marvel of its day, had been thrown almost two miles across the St. Lawrence to Saint-Lambert.

Trains actually began using the bridge late in 1859. But so proud were Montrealers of their achievement that, earlier in the year, they had invited Queen Victoria to journey all the way to Canada and inaugurate it officially. Perhaps they didn't really believe she'd accept. Certainly, few were disappointed when, in declining, she said that in the summer of 1860 she would send her eldest son, the future King Edward VII, to do the job instead.

The eighteen-year-old Prince Albert had much to look forward to on his four months away from home. Notably, there was the laying of the cornerstone for the new Parliament Buildings in Ottawa and a long swing through the United States that included a spell as President James Buchanan's guest in Washington. But one of the undoubted highlights was his week in Montreal.

The prospect of his visit sent everyone in the city into a flurry of activity. The riverside facade of Bonsecours Market, where the prince would step ashore, was finally finished. Several long-gestating housing projects, including the elegant Prince of Wales Terrace on Sherbrooke Street, were also completed. Roads were paved, dressed-stone walls replaced rude fences. Fountains were built, and Montreal's first mailboxes were set up. Sumptuous new robes of office were ordered for Mayor Charles-Séraphin Rodier. The Board of Arts and Manufacture commissioned an exotic-looking exhibition hall, the Crystal Palace, for Ste. Catherine Street at McGill College. City council authorized the building of a vast—though temporary—circular pavilion that could hold thousands of people on a site a little to the west at Peel Street.

Nearly a dozen ceremonial arches, gaily decorated and rising as high as sixty feet, were erected over the principal streets. Gaslight was rushed into service everywhere, it seemed, to make of it all a fairyland by night, so much so that an apprehensive gas company warned householders not to go overboard, lest the system break under the strain.

At last it was August 25, a Saturday. The newly refurbished side-wheeler *Kingston*, with the royal party on board, arrived from Quebec City. But despite all the planning and preparation, things instantly threatened to get off on the wrong foot. Steps had been built down from the Bonsecours Wharf to the water, on the understanding that the prince would come ashore from the *Kingston* in a small boat. The prince or his handlers had other ideas. The *Kingston* would draw up to the wharf itself: the scarlet-draped steps had to go.

If the throngs of ordinary Montrealers squeezed around the market building were merely mystified over what was happening, the official welcoming party were surely mortified. Various bishops and other clergy, a stern phalanx of military officers and Mayor Rodier in his new crimson robes, attended by his councillors, shifted impatiently from foot to foot. Finally a gang of workmen was rounded up and pointed toward the offending structure.

"The exceedingly great haste and bustle of the men to remove the steps, seeing that the Prince was waiting, did not at all increase the speed of their operations, as such things seldom do," a witness recorded, "and this made the scene very amusing." Fortunately for Montreal's *amour propre*, the prince shared in the amusement. Far from taking offence at the near-fiasco, he "could not forbear from laughing outright, and he was seen to exchange good-natured words with the Duke of Newcastle." No *lèse-majesté* here.

Finally the steps were gone. The *Kingston* drew up to the wharf, and the prince and his entourage stepped directly ashore. The weather was cool, but the reception was not—despite the delay. Tens of thousands of people at the waterfront and then along the ceremonial route uptown cheered themselves silly. The Crystal Palace, with its exhibits of minerals and other raw materials, manufactured goods and even artwork, was duly opened. Later, in the afternoon, it was on to the new bridge, the main object of the whole exercise.

The official party arrived at the bridge's north abutment on special rail cars. The prince was handed a silver trowel, its handle shaped like a beaver, and he quickly smoothed out the mortar that had been spread on a six-ton block of granite. This last stone was slowly lowered a couple of feet to its final rest, and the prince ceremonially tapped it into place with his trowel. The party was then chugged to the central span of the bridge where the prince drove in the final rivet. Perhaps by design, certainly by inclination, the speechifying there was brief. The bridge when first built was enclosed, with a steel roof above and steel walls on either side, and the prince and the others suffered cruelly from the smoke pouring from the halted locomotive.

Albert was staying at the elegant mansion of Sir John Rose, which stood on the side of Mount Royal where Percy Walters Park is today. That evening, the streets of Montreal were thronged with people anxious to see the festive decorations. The young prince wasn't going to let the day's tiring activities hold him back, but nor was he anxious to endure more cheering and waving. He ordered up an unadorned carriage, put on a droopy hat to hide his features and set off to join the fun.

He was accompanied by the august General Sir William Fenwick Williams, a Canadian-born hero of the Crimean War and military

Grand finale of fireworks in honour of the Prince of Wales and the
successful completion of the Victoria Bridge.
(G.A. Liliendahl, *Harper's Weekly*, September 1, 1860.)

The Prince of Wales lays the last stone of the Victoria Bridge.
(*London Illustrated News*, October 6, 1860.)

The Prince of Wales stayed at the elegant mansion of Sir John Rose, which stood on the side of Mount Royal where Percy Walters Park is today. (Library and Archives Canada)

commander of all British forces in North America. Unfortunately for their excursion, however, Mayor Rodier had banned vehicles from the streets that evening, the better to let people stroll freely about. As the carriage turned into Rue Notre-Dame, a punctilious constable stopped them. No, no, the coachman protested, but the constable was unmoved. But the prince himself is inside, said the flustered coachman. The constable, "putting his finger to his proboscis," still wasn't buying it— and thus, though inadvertently, did Montreal once again thumb its nose at royalty.

People in the street overheard the exchange and, unlike the constable, believed what the coachman had let slip. They started to unhitch the horses from the carriage; in their excitement, they would pull the prince and the general through the streets themselves. But the coachman, his wisdom matching his skill, managed to turn around and head back up the mountain. The impromptu excursion was over.

On the Monday, there was lacrosse to be watched and a levee at the courthouse to be conducted. But the highlight was the magnificent ball that evening in the temporary structure on Peel Street.

Temporary, yes, but not slapdash. On a site where cattle had grazed just five weeks before, there now stood a magical building that measured more than 900 feet around. It was Coleridge's stately pleasure dome come to Montreal. Inside, at the very centre of the circular structure, there was a raised platform for the orchestra, surrounded by a vast dance floor, which in turn was surrounded by a gallery where guests could pause and watch the dancers. A special section of the gallery was reserved for the prince and his party. Draperies, flags and ornamental shields, as well as painted signs of the zodiac and "reclining female figures," were part of the decorations.

Outside, the effect was just as magical. Flags fluttered from towers attached to the building, making it look castle-like. Lights, some hanging in the trees, lit the surrounding gardens in a jewel-like glow. A stream passed beneath a rustic bridge to feed a pond, and somehow the organizers succeeded in illuminating even the water lilies floating in it. Champagne and claret, we are told, bubbled from fountains. Perhaps it did.

As many as 5,000 people managed to acquire tickets. Some arrived in their own carriages; others relied on cabs, and as the number of available cabs declined, the prices charged by the delighted hackmen went up. Such was the flood of people, however, that soon there were no cabs to be had at any price, and the clunky, horse-drawn omnibuses used to pick up hotel guests at the harbour wharves or the railway station were pressed into service.

Somehow, everyone managed to get there by 9:30 or so—etiquette forbad anyone to show up after the prince did—and promptly at ten the guest of honour arrived. He was hedged in by his suite, including the formidable Duke of Newcastle, secretary of state for the colonies and, in effect, the prince's chaperon. But he was still a teenager, albeit a Victorian one, and he was in a mood to party. There were more than twenty places on the prince's dance card, and he filled them all but the last. At four a.m., he was still on his feet.

Lest offence be given to the ladies of Montreal or tedium be suffered by the prince himself, he was to have a different dancing partner each time. But it didn't work out that way. One of his first was a certain Miss Napier, and lo! her name appears on his card near the close of the ball as well. Did she catch his eye as no one else could manage that night? Indeed, did they see more of each other as the week wore on? Sad to say, we will likely never know.

To be sure, not everyone was pleased with such bacchanalia. The *Montreal Witness*, a dour newspaper of Methodist outlook, inveighed against the succession of lavish balls being held during the prince's tour, and not just for their corrupting effect on the young prince himself: "Churches, ministers and parents will, we fear, find their difficulties about dancing and late hours greatly increased; and many persons will be led, by high example, into this seductive gaiety who might otherwise have resisted the temptation."

But if the prince was in danger of debilitation, physical if not moral, he wasn't showing it. Later that Tuesday morning, after a mere two hours of sleep, he was roused for an excursion by rail to Dickinson's Landing, just west of Cornwall. This would be followed by an exhilarating return on the steamer *Kingston* through the Long Sault and Lachine rapids back to Montreal. On Wednesday, there was a military review at Logan's Farm, today's Lafontaine Park, after which the prince was taken to Dorval Island for a picnic.

A canoe excursion organized for the Prince of Wales passes Kahnawake.
(Watercolour by Frances Anne Hopkins, 1860.)

And what a picnic it was. Sir George Simpson, the North American governor of the Hudson's Bay Company, had owned a house there for several years. Sir Fenwick Williams, who had accompanied Prince Albert on Saturday's attempted night on the town, was renting the property and would be the prince's nominal host, but it was Simpson who laid on the excitement.

The royal party was met at Lachine by two barges that took them the last lap to Dorval Island. As they approached, a brigade of birchbark canoes suddenly swept out from behind the island, seemingly to cut off their passage. The paddlers were Mohawks, "costumed *en sauvage*, gay with feathers, scarlet cloth and paint," and chanting "the inspiriting cadences" of voyageur songs. Just when it seemed there must be a collision, the canoes parted with military precision, leaving a passage through which the prince's boat could glide.

Prince Albert was delighted. With the Mohawks alongside, he arrived at the island to a round of cheers that he "returned by saluting his Indian escort."

Lunch by comparison was staid, with some forty-odd guests, most of them laden with wealth, titles, honours and whiskers. "No one was allowed to be (present) who could not meet His Royal Highness on terms of social equality," a newspaper reported.

After lunch, the prince himself was to go canoeing. When the moment came, he and some of the more adventurous whiskers stepped into canoes waiting at the shore, and they were off. Flags fluttered from the canoes, the royal standard from the prince's. The Mohawk paddlers headed back toward Lachine and then, with Simpson himself directing the show, they swung across the head of the rapids to bear toward Kahnawake on the far shore.

A watercolour by Frances Anne Hopkins, whose husband was Simpson's private secretary, captures the colourful scene. The picture, now in the queen's possession at Windsor Castle, shows it all: the canoes with their flags, a man in a rowboat tipping his hat in salute as they passed, people crowding the shore, the little church at Kahnawake in the background. And even when they got back to the Montreal side, the excitement was not over, for once again the faithful *Kingston* was called on to shoot the rapids and convey Prince Albert back to the city.

So successful had Monday night's ball been that in the evening a second "people's ball" was held at the Peel Street pleasure dome. Ticket prices were reduced, people weren't obliged to dress formally and the prince even put in a brief appearance, though he did not dance. Perhaps the mysterious Miss Napier was not there to tempt him. On Thursday, there was a day-long excursion by train over the new bridge to Sherbrooke and back, and on Friday the royal tour moved on to Ottawa.

Montrealers talked about the royal presence for years afterward. What they also talked about—though more likely in whispers, and only in the upper reaches of society at that—was how they might have had royalty among them all along.

Though they weren't related, Sir Fenwick Williams shared more than his surname with the unfortunate Eleazer, the would-be king of France. Like him, though with rather more cause, General Williams believed himself to be of royal blood. From the day he was born, people suspected he was the illegitimate son of the same Prince Edward who had briefly seen Montreal in 1792. Edward also being Victoria's father, this would make the general nothing less than a half-uncle to the Prince of Wales.

Surely no one at Sir John Rose's mansion the evening the prince arrived in Montreal, or at the Dorval Island picnic four days later, would have been so ill-mannered as to have said anything out loud. But if people had been inclined to search for Bourbon hints in the features of Eleazer, they certainly would have been looking for Hanoverian ones in Fenwick's. Throughout his long life, the old soldier enjoyed the rumours and did nothing to discourage them. For anyone seeing the general and the prince side by side that week in Montreal, the temptation to search for a giveaway timbre in the voice or cast of the nose would have been irresistible.

Williams was born in 1800 in Annapolis Royal, Nova Scotia, as the son of Thomas Williams, commissary general and barracks master of the British garrison at Halifax. But concerning the new baby's true parentage, many in that tight-knit garrison community thought they knew better. And perhaps they were right.

Six years before, in 1794, Prince Edward found himself in Halifax where he took up an appointment as British commander in Nova Scotia and New Brunswick. In 1799 he was created Duke of Kent and named commander-in-chief for North America. He was as insistent on military decorum as he had been in Quebec, and let it be known he didn't think much of looseness in civilian life, either. But for many, there was a whiff of hypocrisy in his professed morality, not least because of Julie's irregular status.

Then there was his friendship with Thomas Williams and, more particularly, his wife, Maria. Was it just that with Maria, mere friendship?

Certainly in August 1800, when Kent left Canada to become governor of Gibraltar, she was well and truly pregnant, and Fenwick was born four months later. Kent was never to return to Canada and, unlike his licentious older brothers with their numerous illegitimate children, he never publicly acknowledged any such legacy, certainly in this country.

The young Fenwick joined the British army at the age of fifteen and Kent, until he died four years later, is said to have kept a watchful eye over his career prospects. Certainly, Williams advanced steadily enough, despite the post-Napoleonic doldrums afflicting army appointments.

He eventually found himself stationed in Turkey. When the Crimean

War broke out in 1854, with Britain and France opposing Russia, he was assigned to help the Turks reorganize their army. The following year, at the town of Kars in Turkey's northeast, he settled in to defy an invading Russian army. After a five-month siege, with no prospect of reinforcements and with disease rampant in the town, Williams knew he had to surrender. But such had been the grit and skill of his defence that the Russians allowed him and the surviving garrison to march out with full military honours.

He spent the remaining months of the war as a prisoner in Russia before returning to England a hero. He was knighted, promoted to major-general, elected to Parliament, and given a pension of £1,000 a year for life. After a stint as commander at Woolwich, near London, he was sent out to Montreal in 1859 where he was to set up his headquarters as commander of Britain's forces in North America. It was the same job his putative father, the Duke of Kent, had held sixty years before. By another coincidence, in 1870 he acquired yet another job once held by Kent when he, too, became Gibraltar's governor.

Throughout her long life, Queen Victoria was not amused by rumours of bastards, the general among others, whom her father might have sired, and did what she could to suppress them. The stories have lived on, nonetheless.

Not all the royals who have come calling on Montreal have been British. Indeed, the first of these exotics had the added disadvantage, at least in the eyes of royalty snobs, of a birth just two generations away from the common herd. Prince he was, nevertheless, and a French one at that, no small consideration on the shores of the St. Lawrence.

It was September 1861 when Napoléon-Joseph-Charles-Paul Bonaparte arrived in Montreal. Known as Prince Napoleon, he was a cousin of Emperor Napoleon III, a nephew of the great Napoleon himself and, until a son was born to his cousin in 1856, the heir presumptive to the imperial throne. In appearance as well as name, he was Napoleonic: short and tending to stoutness, with a characteristically pouting, square face. Yet his handwriting was rather delicate. "The autograph of Prince Napoleon," *The Gazette* reported, "consists of the word Napoleon, written in small letters, and almost in a feminine hand, and immediately under it Jérôme in equally small letters, enclosed in brackets." (Jérôme was a name he assumed in 1847.)

The prince had set out two months before primarily to tour the United States. His itinerary included a visit to the Great Lakes region, which had been part of New France, so a detour to the heart of the former colony was perfectly natural. His visit was a private one, in no way at the behest of the French government, though if his reception in Montreal was vastly less spectacular than the Prince of Wales's the year before, it nonetheless was respectful.

Yet the royal toe barely dipped into French waters here. He stayed less than a week, and spent much of his time in the company of the military—the very military, he might have reflected, that a century before had ended French rule in North America. Invited by Sir Fenwick Williams, he inspected a regiment on the Champ de Mars. He dined with General Williams and the cream of his officers. He took a side trip to Quebec City where he toured the Citadel and its famed defences, dined with Governor General Sir Edmund Walker Head, and reviewed the garrison on the fateful Plains of Abraham.

The prince was a soldier, though what his military hosts made of his less than stellar record is not known. Several years earlier, at the siege of Sebastopol during the Crimean War, the tedium of the campaign got to him and he retreated to the bright lights of Paris, only to find the glitter he sought was dimmed by whispers of cowardice. Not for nothing was he known as Plon-Plon, which was said to be a corruption of *crainte-plomb*, or afraid-of-lead. Other explanations for the nickname are scarcely more flattering. Some unkind souls said it meant Mr. Plod; others said it dated from his boyhood, when he was unable to get his tongue around the name he shared with his famous uncle.

He grew up dissipated, impetuous, wanting in tact and—surprisingly, given his princely station—sympathetic to the political left. So when a delegation from Montreal's republican, anti-clerical Institut Canadien called on him at the Donegana Hotel, where he was staying, the prince received them warmly.

The Institut profoundly alarmed the Roman Catholic Church, and three years before Bishop Ignace Bourget of Montreal had placed the contents of its library on the index of publications forbidden to the eyes of faithful Catholics. Undaunted, Peter Macdonell, the Institut's president (despite the Scottish name), and his colleagues made their case. Mixed in with personal flattery, with an added nod to "their ancient mother country" and "the sympathies of a common origin," they let the prince know that their library could use help.

Prince Napoleon needed little further prompting. "I receive with pleasure, gentlemen, this expression of your sentiments," he said, "and will willingly transmit them to the Emperor, my cousin. ... I know the liberal spirit of your Institute which is eminently useful, and pray you to look upon me as one of yourselves. I will be happy to be your intermedium at Paris to procure your new donations of books and *objets d'art*. I place myself at your disposal."

Had events a few years before worked out differently, not only Bishop Bourget but Queen Victoria herself might have been scandalized by the prince's initiative. When France and Britain were allied in Crimea, there was talk of a marriage between Prince Napoleon and Princess Mary of Cambridge, Victoria's cousin. Eventually the queen said no, objecting to the difference in their religions.

However, there might have been another theological objection, however tenuous. On a state visit to Paris in 1854, Victoria found the prince uncomfortably like the Devil himself, his conversation "disagreeable and biting" and his smile "quite satanic." Had he only sounded more pleasing and looked less Mephistophelian, Montrealers might have entertained not only a French prince in 1861 but at the same time a sort of English one as well, if only by marriage.

In 1876, the city was host to the splendidly named Dom Pedro de Alcântara João Carlos Leopoldo Salvador Bibiano Francisco Xavier de Paula Leocádio Miguel Gabriel Rafael Gonzaga de Bragança e Borbón. Otherwise known as Dom Pedro II of Brazil, he was the first reigning monarch to set foot in Montreal.

Unlike the hapless Eleazer Williams, he was genuinely descended from the Bourbons of France, to say nothing of several other royal houses including those of Britain and Portugal. Unlike Plon-Plon (and despite the New World site of his empire), he was no royal parvenu.

Dom Pedro was then fifty years old, full-bearded, looking remarkably like some older brother of Alexander Graham Bell. Indeed, in Philadelphia that year, he met Bell and tried out the inventor's newfangled device, the telephone. "To be or not to be," he recited, and when the famous Shakespearean line instantly emerged from the other end he exclaimed in astonishment, "This thing speaks!"

His visit, like Plon-Plon's, was not an official one, but merely part of a private tour, mainly of the United States. He was particularly susceptible to the smell of greasepaint, and reserved a box at the Academy of Music for the duration of his brief stay in Montreal. He arrived by steamboat on the evening of June 6, rushed with his entourage to his suite of rooms at the St. Lawrence Hall and, "after arranging his toilet," proceeded to the theatre.

The first act was well under way when he arrived, but the title of the play, *Pique*, in no way described the audience's reaction to the interruption. The play was halted, the national anthem was played, the audience applauded enthusiastically and the emperor graciously signalled his thanks. Dom Pedro was exotic, but he was also royal.

Another exotic was the irrepressible Queen Marie of Romania, who arrived in October 1926. Like so many occupants of European thrones, she was one of Victoria's grandchildren. In fact, cousinhood being no bar to marriage, especially a dynastic one, she was strenuously wooed for a time by another of these grandchildren, the future George V of Britain. Marie's mother, the daughter of a Russian czar, loathed her English in-laws and put the kibosh on any engagement. Marie was eventually made to settle for the Romanian crown prince, Ferdinand.

Certainly the fifty-year-old Marie was beautiful, as she didn't shrink from reminding people. "I am said to be the most beautiful woman in Europe," she fearlessly stated. "About that, of course, I cannot judge. ... But the other queens I know, and I am the most beautiful queen in Europe." On another occasion, she decreed that "fashion exists for women of no taste, etiquette for people of no breeding." Just a week before arriving in Montreal, she was at New York city hall where Mayor Jimmy Walker, a notorious lady's man, dramatically paused before pinning a medal to the queen's sumptuous bosom. "Proceed, Your Honour," she said. "The risk is mine."

"And such a beautiful risk it is, Your Majesty," the dapper Walker replied.

Prone to lines like that, no wonder she sometimes made her English relatives cringe.

Her drawn-out progress through the United States and Canada, with its Montreal stopover, must have been a trial for those stuffed shirts. Not to put too fine a point on it, she was begging. Romania had been shattered by the First World War, and almost a decade later had scarcely begun to recover. The queen hoped that her charm would help produce some much needed aid from her adopted country's one-time allies. To that end, she most unroyally talked to U.S. and Canadian reporters whenever she could, and even wrote a newspaper column titled Queen's Counsel, which the *Montreal Standard* was pleased to carry.

Hours before her train drew into Montreal's Bonaventure Station, a red carpet was rolled out and the people waiting to see her, young and old alike, delighted in tiptoeing along its length whenever the police on guard turned their backs. Finally, at 9:30 that morning, the carpet was put to its intended purpose. The queen stepped down from the train, closely followed by one of her sons, twenty-year-old Prince Nicolas, and his younger sister, Princess Ileana. A forty-mile motor tour of the city was laid on, with stops at city hall, the Université de Montréal and McGill University, and the clapping and cheering along the route were enthusiastic.

Yet there were a few hiccoughs along the way. At one point on Sherbrooke Street, an overzealous cop on point duty held up the royal procession to allow a cart loaded with planks to cross on its ponderous way northward. The police escort often sped ahead, and on several occasions the cars in the motorcade lost contact with one another. The result was that the queen's car, arriving first at some destination, had to idle while the others raced to catch up before the planned ceremonies there could proceed.

For all Marie's regal airs—witness the extravagance of her gowns and jewellery—she was able to soften them with a more common touch. If that was what it took to advance Romania's prospects, she doubtless thought, then so be it. "Throughout the streets her progress was greeted with cheers and clapping from young and old, rich and poor alike," *The Gazette* reported. "School children and greybeards, fur-coated women and white-aproned butcher boys all fell captive to her charm." In the downtown business district, "office boys perched perilously on architectural protuberances" while windows were black with more dignified members of the firms.

Prince Nicolas's common touch was less assured. "You know high hats gag me," he said, while slipping away from the official tour for an unofficial one of the Turcot Yard roundhouse. From there his Canadian National Railways hosts whisked him downtown to a waiting electric locomotive, which he was allowed to drive through the Mount Royal Tunnel all the way out to Cartierville and back. Playing at an engine's controls was more to his taste than shaking hands and waving to crowds.

His disappearance was especially felt by Montreal Romanians who had gathered at their Church of the Annunciation of the Holy Virgin on Rue Rachel to greet the royal party. Far from wearing top hats, many were turned out in Romanian national dress. One of them, a man named Trahan Cabba, in decorated smock and white pantaloons, was to present the prince with a gold-headed cane engraved with his country's arms.

The queen duly arrived at the church, her daughter as well; but nowhere was Prince Nicolas to be seen. After a brief religious service, the royal ladies and their entourage departed. Cabba was practically in tears. It was left to a newspaper photographer to do what he could to soothe the hurt feelings. First, in front of the church, he lined up everyone he could find who was wearing national costume. Then he placed Cabba front and centre. The spurned patriot, reviving, "gleefully waved the cane as the celluloid immortalized the proceedings."

Whatever Marie's visit to Montreal did to preserve Romania and its monarchy, it certainly inspired perhaps the least distinguished verse ever written by Frank Scott and A.J.M. Smith. Then students at McGill, these emerging high priests of modernist poetry greeted her visit to the campus (as well as escape artist Harry Houdini's the week before) thusly:

> *Masses shouted for the Queenie,*
> *Masses shouted for Houdini.*
> *Did you ever see such asses*
> *As the educated masses?*

Royal exotics are all very well. But the royalty that has truly counted for Montrealers has been the undiluted British article. This the city got in spades from Edward, another Prince of Wales. Over the years this grandson of the prince who came in 1860 would be in Montreal half a dozen times. Some of the visits were official ones, met with loud public acclaim; on others, he was just passing through on his way to his ranch in Alberta.

He visited Montreal for the first time in the autumn of 1919, and was idolized. He was good-looking, a war veteran, unmarried, and the future king. We also know, today, that he was selfish, easily bored, often immature, often contemptuous of those who looked up to him, carrying on with married women (notably Freda Dudley Ward, the estranged wife of a prominent Liberal MP), and not very bright. Only occasionally was this less attractive side apparent, but few in Montreal had eyes to see it.

One of his first official duties here was to unveil the new war memorial in Notre Dame de Grâce Park, possibly the first to be erected in Canada since the Great War's end less than a year before. The park was crowded with people as his motorcade pulled up. Many of those waiting were schoolchildren with small Union Jacks fluttering in their hands.

Also waiting was a group of four war veterans in uniform. They seemed distracted, somehow not connected to the bustle around them, their gazes averted even as the prince approached. Pausing in front of them, the prince held out his hand to be shaken. Nothing happened.

They were blind, of course. The prince's hand could not be seen, and no snub was intended. Nor was any perceived. With great tact, the prince said, "Now let me shake hands with you." And so he did. The incident was a small one, but what might have been an embarrassment became a minor triumph.

Afterward, the prince's motorcade started for downtown along Décarie Blvd. A teenager, Berthe Lefebvre, was standing on the curb holding a white rose when Edward's car happened to slow to a crawl in front of her. She didn't hesitate. According to a newspaper report, she stepped onto the car's running board, handed the rose to the prince, then somehow managed to kiss his fingers as he took it. "The prince smiled and waved as the car drove off," the newspaper said, "the whole affair taking much less time than it takes to tell."

For anyone seeing the incident that way, it was another example of his ability to connect with ordinary people. Yet in truth Edward was offended. In a letter to "my vewy vewy own darling precious beloved little Fredie Wedie"—that is, Freda Dudley Ward—back in England, he complained that "a proper little beta of a flapper (aged fourteen to sixteen) jumped up on the car this evening & clung to me with an iron grip imploring me to kiss her, curse her!! Needless to say one of my 4 trusty marine orderlies pulled her off gently but firmly & she was never near gaining her objective, thank God!!"

We can only wonder what he might have written to Freda had he seen "A Tribute in Habitant from Jean Baptiste Canuck," fifty lines of eye-rolling doggerel that appeared in *The Gazette* that week. It began:

> *Bon jour ma frien'! I s'pose you're go'*
> *To see de Prince to night.*
> *An' I can tole you "right off bat"*
> *D'at's be de ver' fine sight.*

Modesty led the poet to sign himself merely as L.D.E. He had much to be modest about.

Certainly the prince didn't think much of French Canadians. They were "mostly a rotten priest-ridden community who are the completest passengers & who won't do their bit in anything & of course not during the war!!" His courtesy visit to Archbishop Paul Bruchési—"the old R.C. Bishop of Montreal, who is laid up with a skin disease"—also tried his patience.

Jews didn't fare any better. Sir Mortimer Davis, the tobacco magnate, was a "revolting fat opulent ... tobacco king & 'nouveau riches' personi-fied!!" The prince was happy enough to use Davis's Rolls Royce, which had been put at his disposal, "though I resent being under an obligation to the bounder." At least he was able, unreservedly, to admire the palatial Davis residence on Pine Avenue when he dined and danced there.

In the summer of 1927, Edward was back in Montreal, this time accompanied by his younger brother Prince George and Britain's Prime Minister Stanley Baldwin. They were touring Canada as part of celebrations marking the diamond jubilee of Confederation. As usual, the crowds were ecstatic wherever he went; and, as usual, there were signs that his heart was not entirely in it.

The prince stepped ashore from a river steamer, just as his grandfather had done sixty-seven years before, and from the Old Port was escorted into the city. As the royal motorcade passed slowly through the cheering crowds, a young woman rushed up and threw something toward the prince. This time it was not a white rose but a flag.

"It fell on the seat of the auto at his side," *The Gazette* reported, "and he turned to pick it up a moment later. He touched his head mechanically with his hand in salute as the auto crossed Ste. Catherine street, and answered the deafening cheers with a tired smile." Tired? Surely from boredom rather than fatigue, for the tour had begun a mere two days before in Quebec City.

The following day, the newspapers printed details of the princes' itinerary. It included a city-hall reception, lunch and five holes of golf at Laval-sur-le-Lac, a garden party in Westmount and dinner that night at the Mount Royal Club. The routes from one venue to the next were also in the papers, and once more Montrealers turned out in their thousands to see the royal visitors pass by.

Those who hoped to see them on the way to the golf course would be disappointed, for the princes intended to play a full eighteen holes, not the announced five. To make sure they'd have enough time, they would get there not by meandering slowly through various neighbourhoods in "the special and sumptuous open car which had been placed at their disposal" but by speeding there directly "in a closed taxi cab." At some intersections, people waited for an hour or more beyond the times announced in the papers for the princes' passage. In the Town of Mount Royal, hearts, bunting and the flags held by schoolchildren all drooped as they failed to show.

As the afternoon wore on, reporters and photographers clustered at the golf course were determined not to be fooled again. The princes were still out on the fifteenth when they began manoeuvring their own cars into line behind the princely taxi waiting at the clubhouse. The princes finally came in, there was a brief ceremony and then suddenly they took off in the taxi. The press were after them in a flash, leaving the bewildered Scotland Yard detectives assigned to royal guard duty behind in the dust.

"The rate of speed at which the Royal pair headed towards the city precluded any attempts to keep a regular orderly line of autos in their wake," *The Gazette* said, "and the competition for places in the fast-moving procession was keen. So keen was it in fact that the Prince of Wales, enjoying a long briar pipe as he chatted with his brother, turned about nervously several times and signalled to following autos to keep greater distance.

"Several times, with sudden stops and sharp curves to complicate matters, accidents were narrowly avoided."

Despite the mad rush, they were late for the garden party.

Scarcely ten years later, Edward had ascended to the throne, then abandoned it. He was succeeded by his brother Albert, who reigned as George VI (not to be confused with another brother, the Prince George of the 1927 tour) and came to Montreal in 1939. It was a royal tour without precedent. Never before had a reigning British monarch been to the city.

George VI was a shy man whose stutter made him even more un-comfortable in public. Sustaining him, however, was a sense of duty so conspicuously absent in Edward. And in Elizabeth, the future queen mother, he had a vivacious consort who won hearts wherever the couple went. The tour was a resounding success.

That was just as well. War was fast approaching, and the British government was anxious to ensure support on this side of the Atlantic for the coming all-out struggle. Pointedly, the royal couple not only went coast-to-coast across Canada but also spent several days in the United States.

On May 18, in the middle of the afternoon, the blue and silver royal train drew into Montreal's Jean Talon Station, and for the rest of the day and on into the evening, everyday life in the city seemed utterly sus-pended. With so many turning out to see the king and queen, who could have been left to man the machinery in factories, to go shopping, to pay attention in school and to do everything else that people normally do?

An estimated 100,000 Montrealers had jammed around the station by the time the train arrived—this, in a city of less than 900,000—and untold thousands more lined the twenty-three-mile route the king and queen would take downtown. The two were the undisputed focus of all eyes. The adoring crowds scarcely seemed to notice the other luminaries, even Prime Minister Mackenzie King and the immensely popular Mayor Camillien Houde, in the open limousines.

They wound through neighbourhoods fancy and plain, French and English. At several points, they passed temporary bleachers set up to help accommodate the crush. In front of Westmount city hall, two elderly women had been waiting for nine hours, complete with campstools and a box lunch, at a prime, curbside vantage point. The cavalcade took in madly cheering schoolchildren, thousands of Catholic ones assembled at Delorimier Stadium, Protestant ones at Percival Molson Stadium. At one point on Sherbrooke Street a group of Mohawks from Kahnawake had assembled. As one newspaper didn't shrink from noting, they displayed "the reserve traditional in the race." Lest there be any further doubt that the times were different, the banner the men held up read, "Welcome to the Great White Father and Mother."

There was a stop at city hall, where the king and queen signed the Golden Book reserved for distinguished visitors. Then it was on to Place d'Armes for a brief ceremony honouring Paul de Maisonneuve, Montreal's founder, and finally to the chalet on Mount Royal for a tea party. It was a calm interlude. Even though the sun was bright, a fire crackled in the chalet's vast hearth as the official party arrived. The first thing the king did after settling into a chair was to light up a cigarette, on which he "puffed heartily." No one could suspect, of course, that lung cancer would kill him thirteen years later.

Remarkably, the police reported fewer street mishaps than on an ordinary day. There were a few falls with broken bones resulting, and several people fainted in the crush, but none was in real danger. The sixty-odd children who managed to get lost were soon reunited with their families. Only one Gordon Sutherland stands out, in a macabre sort of way. The forty-three-year-old, waiting on Peel Street, suffered a heart attack and was dead before an ambulance could get him to the Royal Victoria Hospital.

That evening, more than a thousand people sat down to a lavish banquet at the Windsor Hotel. Splendid gowns and evening dress were everywhere to be seen. Mayor Houde, as host, sat with the royal couple. At one point, the king picked up Houde's notes setting out the order of proceedings for the evening and, tracing a royal finger down the page,

Camillien Houde, Montreal's irrepressible mayor, hosted King George VI
and Queen Elizabeth when they visited the city, May 18, 1939.
(Library and Archives Canada c85091.)

asked him, "Now, did you remember to do that? ... Are you sure you
didn't forget?" Houde threw back his head, guffawed his famous laugh,
then with mock sternness assured the king, "I have forgotten nothing."

On three different occasions, the king and queen stepped onto a
specially built balcony overlooking Dominion Square to acknowledge
the wild cheering of the crowds gathered below. Mayor Houde, irrepressible as ever, said to the king, "You know, Your Majesty, some of this is
for you." An unmistakable whiff of urban legend *à la Montréalaise* clings
to this famous quip—or indeed, put-down. But if it sounds perilously
too good to be true, it's also perfectly in character with Houde and surely
deserves to be true.

George and Elizabeth were still in their *tenue de soirée* when, with
their entourage, they made their way afterward to Windsor Station,
where their train was now waiting. The tempo of the long day was at
last winding down; soon they would be ready for bed, as distant from
other people as they ever likely would be during the tour. They had
separate bedrooms on the train, and to that small extent they would be
away from each other as well. But not entirely: a small sliding panel had
been provided to connect the two rooms, and through it they could
wish each other good night.

Only Montreal's first Prince of Wales, in 1860, prompted the same unambiguous mix of joy and pride that George and Elizabeth managed. It was the royal tour to end them all—in a sense that William Weintraub hints at in *City Unique*, his chronicle of Montreal in the 1940s and 1950s. The 1939 tour, he wrote, was "the outstanding event in a year that marked the beginning of a new era. ... The 1940s and 1950s were years of ferment. They saw the growth of a sophistication which, by 1959, made it hard for Montrealers to credit how innocent their city had seemed only twenty years earlier, how colonial its exaggerated reverence for a king from across the ocean."

To be sure, sophistication was not always in evidence in 1959 when George and Elizabeth's daughter, the present Queen Elizabeth, was in Montreal with Prince Philip for the opening of the St. Lawrence Seaway. A banquet and ball were held in her honour, this time at the new hotel bearing her name. As the queen and her consort entered the vast ballroom, many among the 2,000 invited guests surged madly forward to get a better look. Some even clambered onto chairs, and moments later one evening-gowned woman tumbled spectacularly from her makeshift aerie, taking a table's worth of china clattering to the floor with her.

Worse was to follow. After the five-course dinner had been served, it was time for the dancing, and once again the guests pressed forward, deigning to leave an open space just a few feet square in the middle of the dance floor. RCMP officers formed a wedge to try to move everyone back, to little avail. "We couldn't push them as if they were a street mob," one officer complained afterward. "A lot of them were very influential people." Only after an undignified appeal over the PA system did the throng relent.

Finally, Mayor Sarto Fournier was able to lead the queen to the dance floor, followed by Prince Philip with Fournier's wife and several other couples from the royal table. The queen, clearly not amused with how matters were proceeding, was seen to stare several times at the ceiling. At one point the mayor, unaccountably not chastened by what had gone on before, waved his hand behind the queen's back, inviting other guests to join the dancing. For his pains, he found his hand briefly tangled in the strap of the queen's silver evening purse.

Finally, after about five minutes, the queen had had enough. She returned to her table and appeared to sigh as she sat down. It was the only time she would dance that evening.

Her reception five years later was also blighted. Separatist demonstrators turned out in Quebec City to protest against her presence. On several occasions, with the queen nowhere near, the local police charged, nightsticks flailing. The demonstrators had done nothing more provocative than simply show up. But that was enough for Quebec City's finest, and soon blood from cracked separatist heads was flowing.

Since that *Samedi de la matraque,* the queen's occasional visits to the province have been tightly circumscribed affairs. In 1967 and 1976, with the eyes of the world focused on Expo 67 and the Olympics respectively, she was scarcely in Montreal at all. As *Gazette* columnist Don Macpherson has put it, those two big events "were carefully presented at the time as being held in some kind of international territory that just happened to be within Quebec's borders."

The queen's parents, and her great-grandfather that earlier Prince of Wales, would hardly know the place—in so many ways.

Chapter Three

~

I spy, with my little eye, something. ...
–Children's game

One day late in 1756, a court martial got under way in Montreal. Had its dust settled differently, Canada as we know it might never have come to be.

On trial were two young Virginia militia officers, Robert Stobo and Jacob Van Braam, accused of spying against the French. Their lives hung in the balance.

The brave and resourceful Stobo was a Scot just thirty years old, his Dutch-born comrade a couple of years younger. In July 1754, they had been given to the French as hostages by their commander, George Washington, then a colonel in the Virginia militia, after he was defeated at the Battle of Fort Necessity in Pennsylvania. Stobo and Van Braam were guarantees for the safety of a score of French prisoners whom Washington had taken in an ambush a few weeks before. It was, in effect, the first passage at arms in the Seven Years' War between France and Britain that would lead to the fall of Quebec in 1759.

Shortly after being handed over to the French that July, Stobo was astonished to see several of his captors showing off articles they had obviously looted, contrary to the terms of capitulation signed by Washington, from the cache left behind by the Virginians. A few days later, there was worse: Indian allies of the French showed up brandishing British scalps and wearing British uniform coats, sashes and caps. They dragged along with them a handful of naked soldiers whom they had captured not during the battle but after the surrender, and now were offering these men for sale as slaves.

Stobo was outraged. In his eyes, the French had no intention of upholding their side of the agreement. So far as he was concerned, this released him from his own obligations. Though the French didn't know it, he immediately went back to war.

By then, Stobo was being held in Fort Duquesne, the site of present-day Pittsburgh. He could see that the fort, the key to France's hold on the Ohio Valley, was under-manned and short of food. Surreptitiously, he wrote two letters, complete with a sketch of the fortifications, to urge an attack. He entrusted the letters to Indian couriers, and eventually they were delivered to British headquarters in Virginia.

Despite the precautions that Stobo took, the French commandant, Claude-Pierre Pécaudy de Contrecoeur, began to suspect he was up to no good. Rather than risking the security of Fort Duquesne any further by having the two British hostages hanging about, he sent them to Quebec City under heavy guard.

There, Stobo was treated with surprising consideration. Officially still a hostage rather than a prisoner of war, he was not locked up. His French improved. He acquired fine new clothes—lace-trimmed shirts, a red satin suit, a beaver greatcoat and a plumed hat—and mingled with the best society that the town had to offer. Even in the salon of Angélique Péan, the Madame Pompadour of Canada, he was welcome. The beautiful and witty Angélique was the mistress of François Bigot, the intendant of New France.

He was allowed to engage in a few trading ventures, travelling on business as far away as Montreal. He was given "the honour of the Mississago Indian nation" in a ceremony in which fish bones arranged like a crown were tattooed on his thighs.

Indeed, in Montreal he actually became a business partner with Luc de La Corne de Saint-Luc, who was not only a well-placed trader and military officer but also a relative of his former captor, Pécaudy de Contrecoeur. This was the same La Corne de Saint-Luc who, in 1773, would figure in the flap over whether church bells should be rung to celebrate the unveiling of George III's bust in Place d'Armes.

And all the while Stobo kept his eyes open, for there he was, travelling up and down the St. Lawrence, coming and going through the gates of the most important fortress in all of New France.

His charmed situation began to unravel a few months later. In the spring of 1755, word was received in Quebec that a London newspaper had mentioned his clandestine dispatches from Fort Duquesne.

He and Van Braam happened to be in Montreal, staying in La Corne de Saint-Luc's house. "Devil of an Englishman," his host shouted at Stobo, "you have written letters. Contrecoeur is furious with you." No longer could the French treat Stobo so gently. The two Virginians were arrested and sent back to Quebec City, where they were locked up in the military barracks.

Further proof of the danger Stobo represented came in July. A new British force under General Edward Braddock had crossed the Alleghenies and penetrated the Ohio Valley—only, like Washington's column the year before, to find defeat. Braddock himself was killed, and in his effects the French found Stobo's letters about Fort Duquesne.

Their trial began on October 20 the following year in Montreal. The governor general of New France himself, Pierre de Vaudreuil, presided. Throughout the trial's three weeks, Stobo maintained that the pillaging by Pécaudy de Contrecoeur's men after Fort Necessity had freed him from any need to honour his own parole. In any event, he continued, the incriminating letter had been written long before war was officially declared in May 1756, making his trial before a court martial illegal.

It didn't work. Van Braam was acquitted (though still held in custody), but Stobo was "condemned to have his head cut off on a scaffold which will be erected for this purpose in the Place d'Armes in this city."

Yet it was far from over for Stobo. Legally, de Vaudreuil was obliged to send the guilty verdict to Versailles for confirmation, and as this could not possibly be returned before navigation resumed the following spring, Stobo's head and body would remain connected, albeit behind bars, for many months still. As it happened, King Louis XV withheld his signature. Perhaps he calculated that by showing mercy he would gain a propaganda victory among allies actual and potential, an advantage outweighing an execution of questionable legality.

Back in Quebec City, however, Stobo knew none of this. He and Van Braam decided to escape. The court he had paid to the likes of Angélique and her circle apparently was not wasted, for obliging friends seem to have smuggled files, chisels and a crowbar into their cell. At any rate, the tools were found there afterward. Then, sometime before dawn on May 2, 1757, the two men forced the lock of their cell. They crept along a corridor, squeezed through a window and jumped, their fall broken by a dung heap below. Their departure wasn't noticed for some hours, for they had bought time with that oldest of prison-escape ruses, a pair of dummies left tucked beneath the blankets.

They were recaptured several days later, but this didn't deter Stobo. He managed to get away a second time, in July, and a second time he was recaptured.

By now he knew he would keep his head, the reprieve having arrived from France. A year passed, yet he remained as determined as ever to escape. Then, with the winter of 1759 loosening its grip, he once again was allowed to walk around Quebec City more or less as he pleased. Why the French should allow this beggars belief. Stobo's memoirs credit appeals to de Vaudreuil by "a lady fair of chaste renown," a "cousin" of the governor whose "heart confessed for this poor prisoner a flame." More prosaically, other British prisoners in Canada were routinely allowed such freedom, so perhaps Stobo was as well—despite his court-proven espionage and his two previous escape attempts.

In any event, it was a case of third-time-lucky. One May night, Stobo led a party of eight other British captives down to the shore of the St. Lawrence where they got into a canoe and began paddling down river. They were bound for Louisbourg, taken by the British the previous summer but some 750 miles away. Along the way, they commandeered a small sailboat and later a schooner and, astonishingly, reached their goal twenty-six days later.

Brigadier Edward Whitmore instantly realized the value of Stobo's knowledge of Quebec, where General James Wolfe was settling in for what was shaping up as a long and perhaps fruitless siege of the city. (Somehow during his escape, Stobo had missed bumping into Wolfe coming upstream.) Stobo was dispatched back to Quebec, where he arrived early in July. Wolfe warmly welcomed him, and no wonder. He had with him a letter from an officer at Louisbourg saying, "Captain Stobo will, I hope, bring you agreeable accounts of the condition of the place and disposition of the French troops, and is able to point out avenues to the place, which will greatly forward your approaches."

Yet Stobo was more than just a behind-the-lines intelligence officer. On July 21, he led a company of 300 men as part of a probing attack on Pointe-aux-Trembles (the modern town of Neuville), eighteen miles upstream from Quebec. Among the prisoners whom the British took were a number of ladies who had sought refuge in the village from the terrible pounding Quebec City was taking from Wolfe's artillery; some, perhaps even the "lady fair of chaste renown," knew Stobo from his days as a prisoner. He took part in Wolfe's unsuccessful attempt on July 31 to establish a beachhead at Montmorency, where he was wounded.

If Stobo's arrival at Quebec heartened the British, it unsettled the French. After the raid on Pointe-aux-Trembles, Louis de Montcalm, commander of the French forces, wrote in his journal, "Who would believe that this man was free in Quebec to the point of being allowed to escape? It is he, they say, who conducted everything, and he is in a position to give a good account of the situation in our colony in all respects."

And so at last the critical question: was it Stobo who told Wolfe about the famous path up the cliffs at Anse au Foulon, the key to one of history's most decisive battles? Was it thanks to Stobo that Wolfe was able to spring so devastating a surprise on Montcalm? The evidence is tantalizing but inconclusive. Stobo's memoirs, almost certainly written by someone else and published thirty years after his death in 1770, make the claim, but of course the man best placed to confirm it, General Wolfe, was killed on the Plains of Abraham on September 13.

It was all over for the French, though the final surrender of Canada didn't come until the following year when three British columns converged on Montreal where de Vaudreuil awaited the inevitable.

Among the approaching British officers, newly promoted to major, was none other than Robert Stobo. Few could have felt the satisfaction he surely enjoyed. On September 8, articles surrendering Montreal were signed by de Vaudreuil, whose signature four years before had condemned Stobo to death. The following day, the remaining French

Governor Carleton reviews his troops in Place d'Armes in 1775 as an American army threatens Montreal. In the left background is the Notre Dame Church that preceded the neo-Gothic edifice we know today. (From *Ville-Marie* by Alfred Sandham, 1870.)

garrison laid down their weapons in Place d'Armes, the very place where his head was to have been struck off. We know that he sought out his old comrade, the newly freed Van Braam, who had been rotting in a Montreal jail on a diet of bread and water. It also seems likely that Stobo at least laid eyes on de Vaudreuil, perhaps even spoke to him. Sadly, we cannot know for certain if he did, even less what might have been said.

Robert Stobo didn't set out to be a spy. Circumstances made him one. But if his work was the difference between success and failure for Wolfe at Quebec, he surely must rank as the greatest this country has seen.

Montreal was then a town of scarcely 4,000 people, on the western edge of European settlement. But if its inhabitants retained any illusions that they were outside the orbit of Great Power manoeuvring, they were mistaken.

Over the next several decades, France would lose its monarchy but not—at least in some circles—the dream of regaining its North American patrimony. Montrealers would see Britain painfully coughing up an old domain, the American colonies, while still trying to digest its new one, Canada. They would feel the new and soon to be mighty United States relentlessly probing toward them from its perch along the Atlantic seaboard.

Treaties could be signed in far-off Europe, but they didn't instantly settle things on this side of the ocean. In Montreal, as elsewhere, the times were ripe for cloaks and daggers. Very heaven it was for foreign agents, secret and sometimes not so secret.

One of the most notable was Benjamin Franklin, sent by the Continental Congress to Montreal early in 1776. The American Revolution had begun the year before and the rebels were anxious to have the people of Quebec join in. With their help, the Americans reasoned, Quebec could throw off the British yoke, too. An American army occupied Montreal in late 1775 and Franklin arrived from Philadelphia the following April. He was scarcely a spy, surreptitiously skulking about; he readily declared who he was and what he had in mind. His mission was to win Montrealers to his cause openly, and to this end was helped by a French-born printer named Fleury Mesplet.

Unfortunately for the Americans, Montrealers, especially French-speaking ones, didn't show much interest in Franklin's appeals. Worse, Mesplet was late in getting to Montreal, having been delayed on his way from Philadelphia when his bulky press fell into the Richelieu River. When he finally did arrive, on May 6, the dispirited Franklin was ready to quit, and did so a week later. The last of the American soldiers withdrew in June, a day ahead of the British who were returning in force up the now ice-free river.

Again, Mesplet was not interested in abandoning his press. He stayed on in Montreal and, despite his revolutionary sympathies, was able to set himself up as a commercial printer. Three years later, he founded Montreal's first newspaper, the ancestor of today's *Gazette*, and it was soon a vehicle for radical ideas like an elected assembly, freedom of expression and an end to religious influence in civil affairs. The back room of his print shop became a meeting place for the town's free thinkers.

One of them, and a frequent contributor to *The Gazette*, was a young man named Henri Mézière. He was born in Montreal in 1771, a little too late to experience the American Revolution as a current event. Not so the French Revolution. So great was its impact on him, so ardent was his zeal, that he resolved to bring this new overturning of the old to Canada.

On February 1, 1793, the infant French republic declared war on Britain and in May, shortly after the news reached Montreal, Mézière quietly slipped away from the town. He travelled rough, as a vagabond, lest he attract attention to himself, and made his way to Mesplet's old base, Philadelphia. There, Edmond-Charles Genêt was establishing himself as the new French ambassador.

The bumptious, thirty-year-old Genêt was proving something of an embarrassment to his American hosts. George Washington, now president, wanted to keep his country clear of the Europeans' war. Yet here was Genêt, making speeches to delirious crowds urging attacks on British shipping by U.S.-based privateers, declaring himself bound to "reunite the brilliant star of Canada to the United States." Other French officials, meanwhile, dreamed not of U.S. expansion like Genêt but of hemming in the United States by reoccupying the old French territories along the St. Lawrence and the Ohio.

Suffice it to say, Canada was in France's crosshairs.

The unexpected arrival of the fiery Mézière, just a few years his junior, suited Genêt perfectly. With more enthusiasm than judgment, Mézière persuaded the French minister that his countrymen were as impatient to overthrow British rule as he was. Genêt duly poured it all into a discourse, *Les Français libres à leurs frères du Canada*, which Mézière was to smuggle back into Canada.

That summer, Mézière set out for Canada with 350 copies of Genêt's letter, plus a few of Thomas Paine's *The Rights of Man*. Though travelling under an assumed name, the newly minted French agent didn't realize that British agents were onto him.

In September, the commander of Fort Ontario—today's Oswego, New York, then still in British hands—could report, "I am informed that a Mr. Mezières (for some time Secretary to Genêt) is now on his way to Canada and, as it is said, with a view of fomenting division among the Canadians." Two weeks later, John Graves Simcoe, the lieutenant-governor of Upper Canada, wrote to his counterpart in Lower Canada, "I have just received Information by a Person of credibility that a French Man of the name of Mazeres or Meziere has been sent by Mons. Genest the French Resident in the United States into Lower Canada. This Emissary is described to me as a young man of great address and properly qualified to disseminate those democratic Principles in which he is a perfect enthusiast."

Perhaps coming to realize he was being watched, Mézière handed over his incendiary papers in upper New York State to one Jacques Rous, who was to take them on into Canada. Rous did so—Genêt's letter was read out in front of a few churches after mass—though with little urgency. Whatever Mézière thought, Rous was no closet revolutionary, and would subsequently become a British agent himself.

Back in Philadelphia, Genêt concluded that more muscular measures were called for. A French fleet returning from Haiti had arrived in New York harbour, and Genêt proposed an audacious plan to his masters in Paris. The fleet would sail to Halifax and burn it, move on to Newfoundland and destroy the British fisheries there, then finally sail up the St. Lawrence and recapture Quebec. Mézière was to sail with the fleet as Genêt's agent.

Thanks again to their own spies, the authorities in Canada learned what was afoot. Fortifications in Quebec, as well as in Nova Scotia, were strengthened and the call went out for more men to enlist in the various parish militias. This call was largely ignored, but fortunately for the British, the sailors on board the French ships were not feeling especially warlike, either. They essentially mutinied against Genêt and, with Mézière still on board, sailed straight for France. There, except for a three-year stretch some years later in Montreal when he repented of his revolutionary ardour, Mézière lived out his days in unrevolutionary comfort. His second wife was a wealthy heiress.

Meanwhile, back in Canada, official apprehensions didn't disappear like the French fleet. The clergy were urged to preach the virtues of loyalty from their pulpits. Rabble-rousers were arrested. Foreigners were obliged to register their presence, and in October 1796 newly arrived Frenchmen were ordered expelled. Rumours persisted of new invasion fleets lying just over the horizon.

Late that year, a prominent Montreal merchant and politician named John Richardson effectively became the chief of intelligence in Lower Canada. He and his agents set about opening mail, questioning suspected radicals and organizing a web of informers to watch for infiltrators from the United States. He became convinced, according to one biographer, that the French were "sending emissaries into Lower Canada to assess the attitudes of the habitants towards France, examine the colony's defences and establish a fifth column to support a naval invasion projected for the summer or fall of 1797."

Into this overheated atmosphere wandered an American named David McLane, entering Canada from Vermont late in 1796. To some he said he was selling wood, to others buying horses. But in Montreal, according to later testimony by a certain William Barnard, he revealed his true mission: to spark revolution. Some months later, in a secluded stand of trees near Quebec City, he repeated this to a man named Charles Fréchette:

"You do not know me, but I have been sent by the French government to incite an insurrection in Canada to deliver our brothers and families from slavery. I am second in command of the French army in charge of operations against this province. I would like to form a corps of Canadiens to take the Quebec garrison by surprise. Tell your brothers, your families about it and perhaps convince them to join with us."

Well, perhaps. There's evidence to suggest McLane had been in touch with Genêt's successor, Pierre-Auguste Adet. Through Adet, he might have learned that a Vermonter, Ira Allen, had recently bought 20,000 muskets, twenty-four brass cannons and other materiel in France on quite advantageous terms, ostensibly to outfit the state militia. The ship bearing Allen and his arsenal was captured by the British, who came to fear the weapons were really intended for an invasion of Canada. McLane, for his part, could have come to believe he was somehow to have a role in that invasion.

More likely, he was a blowhard or a fool badly out of his depth whose imaginings the nervous authorities were in no mood to indulge. He was arrested in June 1797 and tried the following month. Evidence supplied by Richardson supported a charge of treason. No matter that an American could scarcely betray a country not his own: it took just half an hour for the jury to find him guilty.

The judge in Quebec City sentenced McLane to be hanged, then cut down while still alive "and your bowels taken out and burned before your face; then your head must be severed from your body, which must be divided into four parts."

Two weeks later, McLane was taken from his cell and seated on a sled, his back ignominiously to the horse hitched to it. A block of wood and an axe were placed in front of him. He was dragged to the place of execution outside the Porte Saint-Jean where, in front of a huge crowd, he was duly hanged. By a relative mercy, he was allowed to strangle to death before being cut down; only then was he disembowelled and his organs burnt. He was not dismembered, but the executioner did cut off his head and brandish it to the crowd, the grimmest of warnings against the folly of espionage.

Ten years later, Montreal greeted a rather more sophisticated newcomer than poor David McLane. A smooth-talking, Dublin-born rascal named John Henry, he had emigrated to the United States, made some money, studied law, dabbled in politics and was now determined to chance his arm in Canada.

Wealthy, English-speaking merchants in Montreal—men like James McGill, Joseph Frobisher and McLane's nemesis John Richardson—were smitten with him. Several newspaper articles he wrote in defence of the fur-trading North West Company were music to their ears. Another article, attacking President Thomas Jefferson's plans to limit U.S. trade with Britain, appealed not only to the merchants but to government officials as well.

Henry was on a roll. Should war with Britain break out, he told his new friends, the union would crumble and American border states would be only too willing to join Canada. The governor, Sir James Craig, needed no more persuading. In February 1809, he sent Henry on a secret mission back to the States to test how far such separatist thinking had gone. He was given a letter of credence, but was warned to exercise the utmost care in revealing it, no matter how promising someone might appear as a conspirator.

Over the next three months, Henry sent fourteen reports to Richardson that, thanks to a cryptic mark on the envelope, were passed on to Craig unopened. They were just what Henry's spymaster wanted to read: there was little interest in places like Boston in going to war, though in the event of war the northern states would indeed likely secede and apply to Britain for help. Unfortunately for Craig's dreams, it was so much flummery. Henry seems to have met no one of consequence, and drew on newspapers, barroom chit-chat and his own imagination for his reports instead.

Craig might have begun to sense this once Henry returned to Canada. The Irishman's Montreal friends remained steadfast, but the government favours that Henry felt he deserved were slow in materializing. In 1810, he sailed to London where he hoped to do better with imperial officials but, apart from a letter of general recommendation, got nothing for his pains.

On the ship back to Canada, Henry fell in with an operator even smoother then he was, Édouard, Comte de Crillon as well as a knight of Malta, the possessor of vast properties in France and Chile. The count emphasized what Henry already believed, that he was woefully under-appreciated. Why not turn the tables on his ungrateful patrons, de Crillon suggested. Why not sell his papers to the Americans, who doubtless would delight in such evidence of British perfidy?

What Henry failed to realize was that his new friend was not a French nobleman at all but a notorious con-artist named Paul-Émile Soubiron, a man on the run from the French police. Blithely, Henry the one-time secret agent agreed that he now needed a commercial agent, and who better than de Crillon?

In Washington early in 1812, de Crillon found a ready market. The new president, the hawkish James Madison, swallowed the Henry papers whole. Craig's secret instructions and copies of the fourteen reports were just the ticket Madison needed to whip up feelings against his political opponents in New England as well as against Britain itself. Rashly, the president agreed to pay $90,000 for the documents. The sum included the entire U.S. budget for clandestine affairs that year, $50,000, plus another $40,000 to be paid to Henry by de Crillon who in turn would be recompensed later by Washington.

Alas for Madison, the scheme backfired. Congress was distinctly unimpressed when, after receiving the papers on March 9, it was clear they named no names and were woefully short on any specifics of a secessionist plot. The president was made to look like a gullible dolt, squandering money needlessly. Yet the impact of the papers cannot be dismissed entirely, for the War of 1812 undeniably broke out on June 18.

So far as Montreal was concerned, of course, Henry was now a turncoat. He never returned to the city. In fact, a little before the papers were made public in Congress, he discreetly left for France. There he learned the truth about de Crillon. Saint-Martial, an estate in Gascony that de Crillon had deeded to him in gratitude, did not exist. It's unclear how much of the $50,000 payment Henry received, if any at all. Certainly, the collateral de Crillon had given him for a $6,000 loan was worthless. There would be no repayment of the loan, much less of the $40,000 still owed by Washington.

The War of 1812 was mainly fought in three theatres, far south-western Ontario, the Niagara peninsula and the approaches to Montreal. Nowhere was the border between the two countries to change, but without the efforts of two crafty farmers in the Chateauguay Valley, it might have been otherwise.

Charles de Salaberry's victory at the Battle of Chateauguay, against very considerable odds, famously thwarted an American advance on Montreal in October 1813. He won because of the bravery and discipline of his soldiers, as well as through clever diversions like bugle calls in the nearby woods to suggest a larger band of defenders. But he also won because he had a good idea of what the Americans were up to, and that was because of men like Jacob Manning and his younger brother, David.

They were the sons of a Loyalist who had come north after the American Revolution. They farmed near Franklin Centre, just on the Canadian side of the shadowy border with the United States. Like many of their neighbours, on both sides of the line, they had a tidy sideline in smuggling. They knew every inch of the territory.

Several of the local farmers, the Mannings included, had been recruited by the British army to keep an eye on what the Americans were up to. Certainly, there was a lot to see—and to report back to de Salaberry—as several thousand Americans under General Wade Hampton began setting up camp just into New York at Four Corners. They were at the head of the Chateauguay Valley, which led straight northeast toward Lac Saint-Louis and Montreal beyond.

De Salaberry, frantically organizing his defences, was grateful for what his spies could tell him. He knew that American success could well cut the link between Upper and Lower Canada and end the war. But suddenly, on October 3, his flow of information began running dry.

The night before, an American patrol crept up on the Manning farm and surprised the brothers, as well as a friend named Samuel Place, as they lay sleeping.

While the Americans might have been dubious about the Mannings, their main quarry was probably Place. He was already under suspicion as a British spy, and none of the captives was under much illusion about the fate that awaited him at Four Corners. As they were marched along, Place suddenly pretended to be ill. He made for a large, nearby log to relieve himself and, when he got there, rolled over the log and kept on going. When the Americans started to chase after him, one of the brothers shouted that if they didn't come back they—the Mannings—would take off, too.

This sobered the Americans. Fearful of Indian attack, it suddenly didn't seem so wise an idea to go charging off into the bush. The Americans decided to stick with the two captives they still had and drag them along with no more delay.

Notwithstanding their doubts about the Mannings, the Americans were remarkably casual once they got to Hampton's base camp. Far from sending the brothers on, well to the rear, they were confined in a log stable at Four Corners. This made it easy for them to absorb how the American forces were growing. They could guess it would not be long before they were on the march.

Compounding this sloppiness, Hampton was slow to investigate exactly what the Mannings had been up to. Only on October 21, almost three weeks after their arrest, did he get around to questioning them. First, he asked how Montreal was fortified, and got nowhere. Then, not certain where Jacob Manning's true loyalties lay—Manning had in fact been born on the American side of the line—Hampton tried to induce him to ride to the city and scout out its defences. Again, Manning shot back that he wanted no part of the business.

His temper rising, Hampton ordered the two brothers locked up again, and this led to yet another mistake. He failed to realize that the New York militiaman taking them away, a farmer named Hollenback, was a friend of the Mannings whose property lay not far from theirs.

Perhaps loyalty to neighbours was more important for Hollenback than loyalty to his country. Perhaps he simply wanted to shuck the responsibility of guarding his two prisoners. So, heading back to the stable, Hollenback asked Jacob Manning, "Do you want something to eat?"

"No," Manning replied.

"Well, then," Hollenback said, "put for home."

And so, to de Salaberry's later relief, the brothers did.

That day, the Americans crossed the border and began their march on Montreal. They moved slowly, out of caution and because de Salaberry's militias had destroyed bridges and dropped trees across the cart-track. De Salaberry, dug in a few miles ahead, was outnumbered at least two-to-one but, thanks to his spies, had the priceless advantage of knowing how strong his enemy was and where it was marching. He knew, thanks to a report from David Manning, that the Americans had nine pieces of field artillery, a howitzer and a mortar, and that more was probably moving toward the Canadian lines by an alternative route. Hampton had more foes than he realized.

The battle came on October 26. De Salaberry's soldiers and his Indian allies clearly gave the Americans a desperately hot time. The following day, instead of renewing the attack, the now-demoralized invaders began withdrawing back over the border. After another American army advancing on Montreal was turned back two weeks later at Crysler's Farm, near Morrisburg, Ontario, the city was never seriously threatened again.

Four decades later, Montreal was crawling with American spies, not because of renewed conflict between Canada and the United States but precisely because there was no such conflict. The U.S. Civil War was raging, and Montreal was an ideal base for agents of the rebellious Confederate states. Canada was not a party to the war, of course, and Montreal was only a few miles from the porous U.S. border. Slipping back and forth between neutral and Yankee territory was easy. There were Union spies in Montreal, too, doing their best to keep tabs on the Confederates.

There was a certain sympathy in Montreal for the Southern cause. Not that Montrealers had much use for slavery. Rather, many in the loftier reaches of society had grown to know and like the well-mannered, well-to-do visitors from the South who holidayed in the city when summer's heat made their own homes intolerable. Once the war began, this liking spread to the occasional refugees who showed up. And, as the conflict drew toward its bitter conclusion, many Montrealers, like Canadians in general, had another reason to lean Southward: what if the mighty Northern army, once victorious, turned toward Canada to attend to the unfinished business of swallowing up this country?

The Southerners in Montreal liked to gather on St. James Street in the city's finest hotel, the St. Lawrence Hall—so many, in fact, that mint juleps were on the bar list. Some reminisced about the old times not forgotten. Others, as the South's defeat appeared increasingly inevitable, had graver matters in mind, plotting ways to undermine the Union war machine. And on October 18, 1864, who should check in but the well-known actor John Wilkes Booth, a fanatical Southern partisan.

The man who would assassinate Abraham Lincoln six months later in Washington put it about that he had come to arrange an engagement at the Theatre Royal. The theatre was on Rue Côté a few short blocks behind the St. Lawrence Hall, and the hotel pointedly advertised that "several of the best boxes are regularly reserved for the guests."

But during his ten-day stay in Montreal, Booth seemed to spend more time closeted with various Confederate agents than with theatrical ones. Among the Confederates he saw, almost certainly, was the most important of them all, Jacob Thompson. He had been sent north the previous May as the South's chief commissioner in Canada. But Thompson was more than a mere diplomat. Part of his mission was to organize various clandestine operations to help the Confederate cause, and for this he was given a formidable bankroll, perhaps as much as $910,000.

It's not clear whether Booth was formally in Thompson's pay, or was working more or less independently. Either way, there's much to suggest that in Montreal—indeed, in the St. Lawrence Hall—a daring plot Booth had been brooding over since the summer was given new life. Booth would kidnap Lincoln, smuggle him to the Confederate capital of Richmond, Virginia, and hold him as a very weighty bargaining chip for the release of Confederate prisoners of war, even for peace itself.

Booth was remarkably indiscreet as a secret agent. He drank heavily in Montreal, and that inclined him to gab. "Abe's contract is near up," Booth slurred to a companion at billiards one evening. He might have to return to Canada before too long, he continued; he'd have to learn "Canuck airs" because "some of us may have to settle here shortly."

Was it merely coincidence that the day after Booth's arrival in Montreal a mounted band of Southerners made their notorious raid on St. Albans, just over the border in Vermont? There they shot up the town, killing one man and wounding several others, and robbed the local bank of $200,000 before hightailing it back to Canada.

Washington was furious, the Canadian government deeply embarrassed. Soon, fourteen of the raiders were arrested and the following week went on trial. They faced a variety of charges, among them murder, assault and robbery. The judge was Charles-Joseph Coursol who, ominously, was known for his Southern sympathies. He had to weigh a crucial point: were the raiders mere common criminals who could be sent back to the United States, or was the raid a legitimate act of war, making them Confederate soldiers not subject to extradition?

Enter the enigmatic figure of Sarah Slater. Exotic in appearance, scarcely out of her teens, she had been recruited by James Seddon, the Confederate minister of war, to run money and messages to Richmond's cabal in Montreal. Though born in Connecticut, she was fluent in French and a passionate defender of the South.

She was one of several clandestine couriers assigned to go north with papers backing the raiders' claim to be soldiers. She was late getting to Montreal, but it didn't matter. Judge Coursol had already found what he needed in a new Canadian law on extradition. Despite the unusual delicacy of the case, Coursol decided without consulting higher authority that this law had not been properly enacted. The St. Albans raiders, he ordered, should go free. And so they did.

It's likely Slater was also too late arriving in Montreal to meet Booth. However, they were later seen together on several occasions in Washington. Booth's plan to kidnap Lincoln, at a hospital near Washington, was set for March 17 but it came unstuck when the president attended a luncheon at a downtown hotel instead.

What happened next to Sarah Slater is not clear. Some sources say that early in April, she and another Lincoln conspirator, John Surratt, were sent on one last desperate mission to Montreal. They bore a coded message that somehow would have launched a scheme to blow up the

White House, and Lincoln with it. Other sources say she was sent to Montreal to smuggle what remained of Jacob Thompson's Confederate bank account to safety in England. In each of these scenarios, Slater was never seen again; in the second scenario, neither was the money.

In any event, blowing up the White House became largely irrelevant when General Robert E. Lee surrendered on April 9, effectively ending the war. The plot was made totally irrelevant five days later by Booth's shot to the back of Lincoln's head.

A manhunt on a scale never before seen was launched in the United States. Canadian authorities went on high alert, too, for some of the conspirators were said to be making for a refuge in this country. We know that one of them, Slater's travelling companion John Surratt, was able to hide out here for several months. But what about Booth himself?

The accepted version of history is that Lincoln's killer was himself killed after being trapped in a Virginia barn on April 26. But, like John Kennedy's assassination almost a century later, Lincoln's has prompted a seeming infinity of alternate versions.

One of the most compelling hinges on strange doings in Montreal on April 29. Montreal police were tipped off that Booth—until three days before the most wanted man in American history, a man acquainted with the city and who claimed he might one day adopt "Canuck airs"— wasn't dead at all but was staying at the Gareau Hotel, on Rue Saint-Gabriel.

Three Montreal police detectives immediately set off for the hotel. They had photographs of their man. When they arrived, they quietly ordered everyone out, even the manager. Then they closed in on the hotel's reading room, where their quarry was peacefully minding his own business.

The man looked remarkably like the photos and was promptly taken in hand. He protested, but to no avail. He was hustled to a nearby police station where he was searched, then transferred to the Central Police Station in the Bonsecours Market building. There he was hauled before Montreal's superintendent of police, none other than Charles-Joseph Coursol who, in his dual capacity as a judge, had freed the St. Albans raiders six months before.

There was no concerted questioning, no legal process whatever.

Coursol took one look at the prisoner, peremptorily declared he "was not the right man" and ordered him released.

Was it Booth? For years afterward, there were nearly as many Booth sightings as, in our own day, there have been of Elvis. He was in Illinois. In 1866, he met his mother in San Francisco where, improbably, he was setting up in business. He emigrated to Australia. No, he moved to England where, even more improbably, he returned to acting, eventually dying of natural causes in Calais.

Surely this was all nonsense. Yet there remains the curious testimony of Edwin Booth, John Wilkes's older brother and a notably more talented actor. Edwin had gone to live in London where he was able to revive his career, which had been tarred by the scandalous events of 1865. One day, he was in a cab on his way to the theatre. The cab was momentarily held up and Edwin glanced out the window. There, staring back at him just a few feet away, was the face of John Wilkes. The older man leapt into the street and searched frantically about, but nowhere was his brother to be seen. The mirage—if mirage it was—haunted him till the day he died in 1893.

In the years immediately after the Civil War, the Union army didn't march north after all. But invaders bent on capturing Montreal did come, keeping the city on edge for weeks at a time.

In 1866, Fenian raiders thrust into Canada from Vermont and New York State. They were Irish nationalists, and they hoped that by capturing Canada—or at least a good part of it—they could use it as a kind of hostage to gain their homeland's independence. But the skimpy contingents that crossed the border weren't remotely up to so grand a vision, and the large Irish-Canadian minorities, especially in Montreal, showed no interest in coming to their aid. The Fenians were soundly defeated, south of the city at Pigeon Hill near Frelighsburg, and on the Niagara Peninsula.

Then, four years later, rumours of a new Fenian invasion spread, and this time the apprehensions in Montreal were greater than ever. Far from having been taught a lesson, wouldn't the Fenians have learned from their mistakes? Wouldn't they be more ruthless this time, better armed and in greater numbers?

Long a garrison city, Montreal was used to seeing soldiers in the

Montrealers on the Champ de Mars in 1866 cheer local militia units after their return from the U.S. border where Fenians had threatened to invade. (*London Illustrated News*, July 28, 1866.)

streets. But that spring the military presence was even more unmistakable. Local militia units stepped up their efforts to recruit new bodies. Hardly a day went by without one regiment or another parading by, its band bravely leading the way.

The climax drew nigh on May 24. It was Queen Victoria's birthday, and as usual many Montrealers celebrated with fireworks. The racket was an odd foreshadowing of the gunpowder that would soon be going off in earnest. Word had come that the expected invasion was at hand. The Fenians were massing to push over the border from the Vermont village of Franklin, more or less along the route taken in 1866.

That evening, about ninety men from the Victoria Rifles and the Montreal Troop of Cavalry were rushed by train toward the border. Meanwhile, a determined home guard called the Red Sashes of Missisquoi—so called for the sashes they wore across their chests—had dug in on Eccles Hill, just on the Canadian side of the line. They were mainly farmers, local people even less inclined than the Montrealers to yield an inch of their land, especially as some of their shops, houses and barns had been shot up and put to the torch in 1866.

Late the following morning, the Fenians finally crossed into Canada. There were at least 200 of them—some reports say as many as 400—and they considerably outnumbered the defenders. But they hadn't counted on the tenacity of the Red Sashes, whose aim was so devastating that the Fenian advance immediately stalled. Those who didn't retreat to sanctuary in Vermont were kept pinned down by the withering fire.

Later that day, the Montreal units arrived. With their rear secured, the Red Sashes charged down the hill. The now-demoralized Fenians broke and ran. It was all over. The Fenians hadn't learned much from 1866 after all.

Montrealers knew what they owed to the men out in the open on Eccles Hill. But what about the spies, men unknown to them?

One of them was indeed a member of the Red Sashes named S.N. Hunter. Like many people along the border, and like the Manning brothers at Chateauguay in 1813, he counted Americans as well as Canadians among his friends and neighbours. The village of Franklin was as well known to him as Frelighsburg.

During the afternoon of May 23, he got a message from one of these American friends that the Fenians were mustering and might invade in a matter of hours. Hunter decided to see for himself. With another man, he set out for Franklin. It was dark by the time they arrived, and the village was in a frenzy of activity. Strangers could be seen milling about everywhere, many of them armed. He ducked into a local hotel where he bumped into a friend. The Fenians had cached arms all over the village, Hunter's friend told him, including some in a shed behind that very hotel. While they were talking, a wagon careered along the street, its drivers shouting that the green flag of Ireland would soon be waving over all of Canada.

The two spies needed no more persuading. They got back on their horses and, once beyond the lights of Franklin, whipped them home. In Frelighsburg, Hunter telegraphed a warning to the Canadian authorities. Then he rode over to Dunham to alert Asa Westover, the leader of the Red Sashes, who immediately called out his men.

Once morning broke, Hunter ventured back to Franklin. More wagons loaded with ammunition were arriving. The 15,000 weapons and three million rounds of ammunition that John O'Neill, the Fenian commander, is said to have accumulated were certainly an exaggeration, but Hunter could plainly see that the Fenians were impressively armed nevertheless. They even had a breech-loading field gun.

Hunter rode back to Canada to reaffirm what he had reported the previous night. Danger was plainly at hand. And so it was that the Red Sashes were dug in on Eccles Hill well before the raid began.

Not that the Canadian authorities weren't already aware of the threat to Montreal. They had been for some time, thanks to another spy who, remarkably, was at John O'Neill's right hand.

This secret agent was Thomas Billis Beach, a twenty-eight-year-old Englishman who, in his teens and posing as a Frenchman named Henri Le Caron, had drifted to the United States in search of adventure. He met O'Neill during the Civil War while both were serving in the Union army. After the war, Beach allowed himself to be drawn into the Fenian organization. Perhaps he was just curious, but if curiosity it was, loyalty to the land of his birth soon took over. Beach secretly contacted the British government which in turn passed him on to the Canadians. Thanks to his steady stream of reports over the next several years, Ottawa always had a pretty clear idea of what the Fenians were up to.

The 1870 raid was originally planned for mid-April, but when O'Neill received reports of unusual preparations on the Canadian side of the border, he concluded, rightly, that there was a spy in the Fenian hierarchy. Wrongly, he never suspected his old comrade in arms. Another man was denounced as the traitor instead.

Indeed, when the drive on Montreal was finally fixed for late May, O'Neill blithely made Thomas Beach quartermaster in charge of the raiders' munitions. Once the raid got under way, the secret agent did everything he could to sabotage it. He removed the breechpiece of the invaders' field gun and hid it. He delayed the deployment of the Fenian reserve force. And midway through the attack, when O'Neill was suddenly arrested by a federal marshal for breaking U.S. neutrality laws, Beach passed up a chance to free him. As the carriage bearing O'Neill and his captor charged back from the border, it passed the Fenian base camp.

"I understood the situation in a moment," Beach would later write, "but said nothing. To have given the command to shoot the horses as they turned would have been the work of an instant, but it was not part of my purpose to restore O'Neill to his command."

The Fenians were never seriously to threaten Canada again.

Before the century was out, however, Montreal would once more become a focus for espionage, this time during the Spanish American War of 1898. Immediately after war was declared on April 20 that year, the staff of Spain's embassy in Washington left for home, not directly but through Canada. Led by Ambassador Luis Polo y Bernabe, they first went to Toronto before moving on to Montreal a couple of weeks later.

Polo's staff included first secretary Juan Dubosc and naval attaché Ramón de Carranza, and what had been only part of their duties in the United States, spying, became a full-time job once they had left. Unfortunately for them, the spies were spied upon. U.S. Secret Service agents, with Ottawa's tacit consent, were able to keep close tabs on the diplomats' activities in Canada.

The two Spaniards set about monitoring newspapers in earnest. They trawled for information through Montreal's large shipping community. And, perhaps not fully realizing how closely he was being watched, Carranza in particular began recruiting a network of informants. Many were disaffected Americans whom Carranza encouraged to enlist in the U.S. forces, placing them closer to the action. Soon Madrid was bombarded with reports of U.S. ship movements, morale problems and plans to invade Cuba and Puerto Rico, then Spanish possessions.

The Spaniards' base in Montreal was the Windsor Hotel. One day, Carranza was briefing a new recruit, George Downing, a former petty officer in the U.S. navy. But the hotel room had a door leading directly to the adjacent room, and there a U.S. agent sat, ear glued to the door, quietly recording their conversation. Downing was arrested in Washington on May 7 and was found hanged in his cell two days later. The official verdict was suicide, but Carranza would always believe that his man had been murdered by his jailers.

On May 21, Polo and his staff finally left Montreal. But as their Liverpool-bound ship sailed down the St. Lawrence, Dubosc and Carranza were able to go ashore and quietly slip back to Montreal and a house they had rented on Tupper Street. Again, however, they were not as stealthy as they would have liked. U.S. agents duly noted their return.

A week later, one of them, apparently claiming to be a health inspector, was admitted to the house. While Carranza was occupied with eating his breakfast, the agent stole a letter he had written to a supposed cousin in Spain.

The letter was immediately forwarded to Secret Service headquarters in Washington. It brought Carranza's superiors up to date on his activities. It described where U.S. navy ships were deployed. Perhaps most unsettling, it recommended that the Spanish navy bombard east-coast targets like Boston and Portland.

It was pure gold, just what the Americans needed to discredit the Spaniards and insist that they be expelled from Canada. It was just what Ottawa wanted as well. Together with the imperial government in London, it was partial to the U.S. side in the war, yet had no wish to compromise the British Empire's neutrality.

Early in June, the letter was leaked to the newspapers, which promptly had a field day. If any editors suspected the translated version enhanced the original's revelations, as seems likely, they didn't say so. This, after all, was the war that gave yellow journalism to the world. Dubosc and Carranza were ordered to leave once and for all. But as for the other side of the Tupper Street coup, no American was charged with housebreaking or theft, nor expelled for espionage.

Not all spying is military, of course. Secret agents with commercial conquest in mind have snooped around Montreal, too, and perhaps the greatest of these was a man named Andrew Duncan Davidson. Had his mission failed, the look and shape of Montreal would be noticeably different today. There would still be houses and shops and schools on the other side of the mountain, but they would not make up one of the city's most notable communities, the Town of Mount Royal.

Davidson was born near London, Ontario, in 1853 and made a name for himself as a wildly successful land promoter in Minnesota and Saskatchewan. He was just the man William Mackenzie and Donald Mann needed.

In 1899, Mackenzie and Mann founded what would briefly become Canada's third transcontinental railroad, the Canadian Northern. They desperately wanted a terminal in downtown Montreal but, sadly for them, the downtown core was already well built up. Acquiring land there, as well as a right of way leading to it, promised to be very expensive.

Henry Wicksteed, the railroad's chief engineer, had an audacious idea. Why not bring the rail line in from the north and punch a tunnel through the mountain into the heart of downtown Montreal? Indeed, why not try making the scheme pay for itself? Instead of merely buying enough land for a right of way, why not buy whole farms and develop a completely new community, a "model city," on the north side?

It was a challenge tailor-made for Andrew Davidson. He had already developed vast tracts of land on the Prairies that the Canadian Northern served. Now his job would be to buy up whatever real estate the railroad needed in Montreal—but in utmost secrecy.

Like a latter-day agent of Moses "sent to spy out the land," he went up his own mountain in Canaan, Mount Royal. From its heights, he could see farmland—relatively inexpensive farmland—rolling away northward to the Back River. He soon learned that options on much of the land that he needed were already held by a local land speculator named Jimmy Maher. The options were set to expire on April 29, 1911. With just a day to go, Mackenzie and Mann agreed to have Davidson tackle Maher.

He had to move fast, yet with stealth so that Maher would not realize how valuable the options really were. The key was a pair of adjoining rooms at the Windsor. Unlike Carranza thirteen years before, however, Davidson would know exactly what was going on in both of them.

Maher was in one room. Davidson set himself up in the other with a real estate agent named F.H. Shaw, a man in his confidence. On no account could Maher be allowed to see who the mystery buyer was. All through the night, Shaw shuttled between the two rooms, carrying offers and counter-offers back and forth. At last, around 6:30 a.m. on the twenty-ninth, a deal was struck.

Together with other farms he carefully bought up, Davidson acquired some 4,800 acres, most of it where the Town of Mount Royal would soon be built. But what of the downtown part of the scheme?

Secrecy was even more important here, for the land was so much more valuable. But secrecy was even more difficult to maintain, for there were so many more sellers, so many more pairs of eyes and ears. It was probably inevitable that the cat would eventually slip out of the bag. And so it did.

First, two Canadian Northern engineers involved in planning the tunnel under the mountain left a book of the plans on a chair in the lobby of their hotel. By coincidence, this hotel stood on the site of today's Place Ville Marie, about where the tunnel would eventually emerge. A hotel employee saw the book and opened it, hoping to see its owner's name. He saw much more, and soon the rumours began to fly.

Then Davidson himself was careless, venturing out one day to verify some distances along the critical city blocks. He was duly spotted, and even more rumours flew. But by then he had acquired the fourteen acres or so that his employers needed. The tunnel was completed in 1918, and the railroad had a site for its downtown terminal.

Sadly, for Mackenzie and Mann, the vast real-estate development they had foreseen for central Montreal, with their terminal at its heart, would be achieved only decades later, and by other hands. But that wasn't Davidson's fault.

To this day, opinion is divided about whether a dozen or so Germans who passed through Montreal in late 1937 were spies for the Third Reich or not. They claimed to be "a group of technicians" on their way to Anticosti Island, in the Gulf of St. Lawrence, to see about building a sulphite pulp mill there. But in fact were they looking for something else, like places where U-boats could hide?

Anticosti was then owned by Consolidated Paper Co., and its logging operations on the island were in the doldrums. When an Amsterdam entrepreneur named Alois Miedl acquired an option to buy the island in July 1937, Consolidated's ears perked up. So did Montreal's, especially when the survey party checked in to the Mount Royal Hotel at the end of November. The men were "outstanding German engineers, forestry experts and accountants," one newspaper reported. A new pulp mill would provide 2,000 well-paying jobs.

Also staying at the Peel Street hotel was a man named William Glyn. He claimed he was a well-travelled correspondent for various American and British newspapers. Shortly after the Germans arrived, Glyn said, he overheard them discussing what they were really up to. It wasn't pulp and paper. In a sensational letter on December 3 to the federal solicitor general, Glyn said the visitors were military officers and fortifications experts. Several were personal favourites of Adolf Hitler himself.

Could German spies have been so loose-lipped, or did Glyn misconstrue some innocent remark? Did he make it all up? Yet the letter could not be ignored, for Germany's warlike posturings as the 1930s drew to a close were obvious. So were Anticosti's sparse population and its strategic location. The island commanded the vital shipping lanes to Montreal, yet there were few potential prying eyes around—just the combination the Kriegsmarine needed for establishing a submarine base.

Soon, the Germans were on their way to Anticosti, and there they stayed for several weeks. They talked to Consolidated Paper's local managers. They headed off to the bush for days at a time and went up for a few flights in a small plane. They took repeated off-shore soundings, not just in the safe anchorage of Gamache Bay at the west end of the island but in little coves all along the island's shore. They even went winter camping, tried some snowshoeing and managed to set fire to one of their tents. By the end of December they were headed for home.

They left behind a lot of excitement that had nothing to do with the prospect of 2,000 new jobs. But despite the agitation in the newspapers and among the parliamentary opposition, the government concluded that selling the island to foreign interests was neither against the law nor a military threat. Then, in September 1938, Miedl's option to purchase expired and with it the prospect of any pulp mill.

But what about a haven for U-boats? Was the idea really so far-fetched? In November 1939, just after the outbreak of the Second World War, a Royal Canadian Navy vessel as well as two RCMP constables were sent to the island. They were to search for food or fuel supplies that might have been cached by the mysterious Germans, but none were found. Nevertheless, in time German submarines did find their way to the waters off Anticosti. From May 1942 to November 1944, they sank twenty-seven ships in the gulf and in the St. Lawrence River itself.

A man named Charlie McCormick was a fixture on the island from 1926 until his retirement almost fifty years later. Among other things, he was the island's game warden, and often the easiest way to get to outlying spots was by horseback. According to McCormick, on more than one occasion during the war he came upon a U-boat surfaced in a remote bay. He'd fire his rifle, taking care to aim at the steel hull and not at any sailors on deck. Then he'd watch with satisfaction as the crew raced below, the diesels started up and the submarine put out to sea once more.

Some years after the war, McCormick received a surprising visitor. He was German, a member of the very survey party that had caused such uneasiness in 1937, and he had returned to the island for some salmon-fishing. Over drinks one evening, McCormick put it to his guest: what had really been going on that December?

The answer confirmed what he had long suspected. The guest claimed to have been a member of German naval intelligence. There never had been a plan to buy the island for its timber, he said. The survey had indeed been simply to find some places where submarines could surface undisturbed, recharge their batteries and make a few repairs. His guest even mentioned the pot shots of some man on horseback, adding how grateful the German sailors were that his aim had been so bad. That McCormick had deliberately aimed at the submarines, not the sailors, didn't seem to have occurred to them.

There's another curious footnote to this tale. Even today, many *Gazette* veterans can remember a colleague named Karl Gerhard. By the 1970s, Gerhard had become a kind of daytime office manager, making sure things ran smoothly in the newsroom, responsible even for such mundane matters as issuing taxi chits to reporters heading out on assignment. He was tall though a little stooped, and wore a moustache. He came across as a kindly man, had a cultured air and spoke English with a perceptible German accent.

He seemed to have been at *The Gazette* forever. In fact, he had joined the paper not long after the German expedition to Anticosti.

In the months following the expedition, with questions being raised in Parliament and newspapers wildly speculating about what was going on, the *Toronto Star* printed an intriguing report. It claimed that a Dr. Emil Karl Gerhard—or Gerhardt—had been part of the expedition and that he was a personal envoy of Hitler, "well known as Der Fuerher's key man in many important missions, among others as his personal agent at League of Nations gatherings in Geneva."

Could this be true? The race was on to find this Gerhard—or at least a Gerhard who would do—and, two weeks later, *The Gazette* was first across the finish line. He was a Montrealer, one Karl R. Gerhard who had emigrated from his native Germany in 1930 at the age of twenty-three. He had become a Canadian citizen late in November 1937, just before the arrival of the Anticosti "group of technicians."

He had taught languages at the University of Western Ontario, he told the newspaper, before becoming head of the Deutscher Bund Canada. The Bund was a completely benign outfit, he went on, interested in culture and not politics. He also was prominent in the Auslands-organisation der Nationalsozialistische Deutsche Arbeiter Partei, the overseas wing of the Nazi party, but in any event had "severed all connection with any German organization" lest his application for citizenship be compromised. Indeed, there is a suggestion he was deposed as the Bund's leader for refusing to obey directives from Berlin.

Whatever prompted this divorce, it was just as well for Gerhard. Despite what he wanted Canadians to believe, the Bund was a Nazi front, active like the Auslandsorganisation in spreading Nazi ideology in this country. Bund members swore an oath that they were "free from Jewish or coloured blood" and even wore swastika armbands at their meetings.

However, there's no particular reason to doubt his denial that he had visited Anticosti with the other Germans. Perhaps no one named Gerhard had.

He insisted that with his newly minted citizenship he was a thoroughly loyal Canadian—and here the mystery deepens, not least because access over the years to secret RCMP files on the Bund has been restricted. As the Anticosti affair faded from the news, some say the dapper young man "who dressed like Bond Street" was co-opted by the federal force. His job was to monitor what other Germans were up to in Canada, and *The Gazette,* so the story goes, was quietly prevailed upon to give him needed cover by hiring him as a reporter.

Several years later, with war raging in Europe and the Pacific, there was a *Gazette* staff picnic on Île Cadieux. John Collins, then a young cartoonist with the newspaper, recalled a happy scene beside the water, with some people in swimming, others lolling "under the trees guzzling beer." Karl Gerhard—the same Gerhard who would be handing out taxi chits three decades later—was also at the picnic. After a time, he strolled by with a considerably older woman on his arm. A guest sitting near Collins, a young woman from Boston, exclaimed, "Oh, isn't that nice. He brought his mother!"

Not quite. "That mother," Collins went on, "was the daughter of an old Montreal German family whom Karl had married to keep out of the concentration camp." In 1941, there were 114 naturalized German Canadians interned at Camp Petawawa for their Nazi sympathies, of whom seventy-four had once been members of the Deutscher Bund. *The Gazette*'s Gerhard, clearly, was not among them.

Recently, a search was made for Gerhard's personnel records at *The Gazette*. Alone among similar files from the period, Gerhard's, to the astonishment of all, was nowhere to be found.

One of the oddest spies Montreal has seen was Werner von Janowski. How could a self-respecting spy service have been so naive in its planning, and its man on the ground so inept?

On the night of November 9-10, 1942, the forty-one-year-old Janowski was landed by a U-boat on the Gaspé coast near New Carlisle. He planned to go to Montreal, claiming to be a Northern Electric salesman named William Branton, and begin transmitting messages to German intelligence in Hamburg. He wound up in Montreal, all right, but not the way he intended.

Early the morning after he landed, Janowski walked into New Carlisle and checked into a hotel. He was carrying a suitcase containing his receiver-transmitter and a briefcase that held $5,000 in Canadian paper money, $1,000 in U.S. gold pieces, a small pistol, a set of spiked knuckle-dusters, a German ID tag and a German soldier's paybook bearing a swastika. There was also a copy of the children's tale *Mary Poppins*, printed in Leipzig and presumably for concocting codes. All in all, it scarcely painted him as a mere travelling salesman.

Certainly, Janowski's presence seemed odd to Earle Annett, the hotel's owner. The stranger said he wanted to stay just long enough to clean up and have breakfast. He claimed he had arrived in New Carlisle by bus, but the first bus of the day wasn't due until noon. He reeked of sweat and diesel fuel, thanks to his 44 days in the U-boat. The banknotes he used to pay his bill had been withdrawn from circulation years before. He left behind cigarettes and a matchbox that had been manufactured in Belgium, though Belgium of course was then occupied by the Germans.

After Janowski left for the train station, Annett phoned the police.

A Quebec provincial officer arrived, boarded the train with Janowski and arrested him before they reached Bonaventure, just nine miles away. That night, Inspector C.W. Harvison (a future commissioner of the RCMP) took over. In the space of scarcely twenty-four hours, Janowski was on his way from being a mere secret agent to a double agent.

He was taken incognito to Montreal where, according to Harvison's memoirs, he was set up in the Town of Mount Royal home of an RCMP interpreter, a First World War German submariner known only as Johnny. Starting in December and for the next eighteen months or so, the RCMP used Janowski to feed a stream of messages to the Germans. The powerful new radio that Janowski and his Canadian handlers used had to be calibrated with great care lest Hamburg suspect it had replaced the 40-watt Telefunken that the German had lugged ashore.

Harvison and company also had to contend with Johnny's neighbours. Johnny already spoke English with a strong German accent, which made him suspicious enough to the neighbours. Added to this, suddenly, were all sorts of mysterious comings and goings through his basement door. Then, when a radio mast was erected outside the house, the conclusion was inescapable: a spy ring had to be at work beaming clandestine messages to Germany.

The neighbours were right, of course, though not in precisely the way they thought they were. Some of them reported their suspicions to the Mounties. So, eventually, did TMR's police chief. Things were threatening to get out of hand; it was time for more subterfuge.

The Mounties told the police chief that they knew perfectly well what was going on. "We went on to explain the Canadian government had asked the force to carry out some experiments with a new type of radio which was being developed in deep secrecy," Harvison wrote, "and that our experiments were being carried out from Johnny's house."

This apparently satisfied the chief, and he agreed to reassure the neighbours, in as discreet a way as possible, that all was well. The whisperings died away.

It's not clear how worthwhile it all was. A week after VE-Day, the *Ottawa Journal* would claim that "the deceiving of the Nazi spymasters in Hamburg was so successful that other German espionage agents (were) lured into betraying themselves to the RCMP." This seems unlikely, for Janowski's radio traffic apparently was essentially one-way. That is, Hamburg transmitted questions to Janowski but nothing more. But the disinformation sent by Montreal to Hamburg would be another matter, and even long after the war had ended Harvison remained persuaded that the deception had worked.

Germany's feeble effort to set up Janowski as a spy in Montreal was laughable compared with what the Soviet Union managed. There was nothing ham-fisted about Soviet efforts during the Second World War, as the famous and totally unexpected defection of Igor Gouzenko in September 1945 so amply shows.

Three years before, Britain began to move its top-secret project to develop an atomic bomb to Montreal. The project's scientists, including some Frenchmen and Canadians, would be closer to similar research going on in the United States, and safe from Luftwaffe bombs as well. The project was code-named Tube Alloys, and in time would augment the Americans' Manhattan Project. Temporary labs were set up in a Golden Square Mile mansion until more suitable facilities became available in a disused wing at the Université de Montréal. Late in the war, the project spread to Chalk River in Ontario.

Meanwhile, with the Soviet Union fighting on the Allied side, it made no sense for Canada to continue refusing the country diplomatic recognition, nor to keep up its ban on the Communist party here. Early in 1943, Soviet representatives began arriving in Ottawa to set up an embassy and get to know Canadian politicians and other leaders. Parties at the new embassy became a hot ticket. The flow of booze was notorious. At one party, the deputy minister of finance became so drunk he passed out.

The Soviet charm offensive was helped by the presence of a Red Army colonel named Nicolai Zabotin. He was good-looking, suave and, especially before his wife joined him, something of a lady's man. He was ostensibly the military attaché but was really a spy, with a staff of several other Red Army spooks, including cipher clerk Gouzenko. The Soviet Union had begun to work on an atomic bomb of its own and had no doubt Canada, Britain and the United States were doing so, too. Zabotin's mission was to find out as much as he could.

One of the Tube Alloys physicists sent to Montreal was a thirty-one-year-old Englishman named Allan Nunn May. Like many who had come of age in the 1930s, a decade with capitalism in decline and fascism on the march, he was attracted to the more humane future that Soviet communism seemed to promise. He joined the British Communist party.

By the time he got to Montreal, Nunn May believed more than ever that the atom's secrets should be shared among all the allies. He could scarcely have been more ideal for Zabotin's purposes. Duly recruited, the Englishman would hand over a variety of details on how the Hiroshima bomb was meant to work, as well as samples of enriched uranium. The Soviets gave him $200 and a bottle of whisky, for which Nunn May naively signed a receipt.

Also seduced was a Montreal chemist named Raymond Boyer. Like Nunn May, Boyer had swum in the progressive currents of the 1930s. He earned a doctorate at McGill University and saw for himself the emerging evil of Nazism while studying later in Vienna. Once back in Canada, he became active in human-rights and similar groups. He never joined the Communist party but was certainly sympathetic to its professed ideals.

He was hired by McGill's chemistry department after war broke out. In addition to his teaching duties, he worked on a new method of manufacturing an explosive called RDX. He helped organize the Canada-Soviet Friendship League and later the left-leaning Canadian Association of Scientific Workers. He was friendly with Fred Rose who became Canada's first Communist MP in 1943 and who would be among those tried after Gouzenko's revelations.

Boyer was not involved with nuclear research. Nor was he motivated by greed; he was, after all, a comfortably-off grandson of the prominent financier L.J. Forget. But, like Nunn May, he was convinced that scientific information should be shared by all the Allies, the Soviets included. Through Rose, who was in close touch with Zabotin, he began passing on the secrets of RDX.

Not that they were all that secret. The McGill lab where Boyer worked was notoriously porous, neither guarded nor even kept locked. There wasn't much security, either, at the Shawinigan plant where the improved version of RDX was being made. In fact, in 1944 Munitions Minister C.D. Howe authorized a tour of the plant by two Russian technical experts, and was even ready to allow some of the explosive to be shipped to the Soviet Union. He backed off only when Britain and

Raymond Boyer and long-time Communist
and social activist Irene Kon, Montreal 1939.

the United States objected.

It's impossible to guess how long Nunn May, Boyer, Rose and the others in Zabotin's network could have kept going. But their idealism, genuine if woefully misplaced, was trumped by the newly acquired ideals of Igor Gouzenko. With visions of Western liberty, to say nothing of Western material comforts, dancing in his head, he slipped away from the Soviet embassy on September 5, 1945, with his cache of incriminating documents. No one quite knew it yet, but this was the opening salvo of the Cold War.

The Canadian authorities bided their time, not sure what to do. The Russians, tipped off by the notorious double agent Kim Philby that

Gouzenko was in Ottawa's hands, could only wait for the other shoe to drop.

Five months later, it did. Boyer was among a dozen people arrested in Montreal and Ottawa on February 15. Under the War Measures Act, they were held incommunicado and denied counsel for weeks. They had no choice about testifying before a royal commission set up to investigate espionage in Canada. And, with the Cold War rapidly heating up, they started going on trial. The preferred charge was flouting the Official Secrets Act, and Boyer's turn came in March 1947.

"The information that I transmitted to Fred Rose was in the public domain," Boyer told the court. The judge didn't buy it, but despite his earnest instructions to the jury Boyer was acquitted. It took a second trial to send him to Saint-Vincent-de-Paul Penitentiary for two years.

Some of the men and women unmasked by Gouzenko's defection were eventually acquitted or had convictions overturned on appeal. But Boyer was one of eleven who went to prison. Fred Rose was sentenced to six years. Allan Nunn May, tried in Britain, got ten.

Nunn May behaved himself in prison and was released after serving six years. Once back outside, meaningful work was hard to find, and it wasn't until 1961 that he won an appointment as a physics researcher at the University of Ghana. He later became dean, and even served as scientific adviser to the government in Accra. He died in 2003.

For his part, Boyer reflected deeply in prison on how Cold War hysteria had shoved due judicial process aside. As well, he could see every day how prison routine was designed to humiliate and dehumanize inmates. Released in 1950, the scientist whom society had called a criminal turned his back on science and, of all things, immersed himself in criminology.

He published several scholarly articles on the subject. He wrote an important book, *Les crimes et les châtiments au Canada français du XVIIe au XXe siècle*—which, incidentally, devotes three pages to his eighteenth-century predecessor in the ambiguities of espionage, David McLane. He was active on behalf of prisoners and political refugees.

Boyer died in 1993. A man he had known behind bars almost half a century before, Ben Jauvin, spoke at his memorial service. "No former prisoner did more for us ex-convicts to put us on the way back into society," Jauvin said. "For him, prison was like a military college, except that you found there a better class of people."

And Nicolai Zabotin? The slipshod surveillance that allowed his cipher clerk to steal the fateful documents and defect had occurred on his watch. It was an intolerable failure in the Kremlin's eyes. Zabotin and the rest of the Red Army contingent in Ottawa were recalled, and several days later his death was reported.

Heart failure was given as the cause, though a bullet to the back of the neck in Lubyanka Prison was widely suspected. Other evidence suggests that he escaped execution but was sentenced, together with his wife and son, to a labour camp.

Either way, the chance given to both Boyer and Nunn May to reinvent themselves was denied their old spymaster.

Chapter Four

∼

If ye have faith as a grain of mustard seed, ye shall say
unto this mountain,
Remove hence to yonder place; and it shall remove.
–St. Matthew

Montreal was founded as a mission colony. The French came to the head of navigation on the St. Lawrence, not to extend the imperial sway of their kings (though that did happen), nor to make money (though some of them soon did). No, at the outset their chief intent was to bring the word of God to the Indians.

Martyrdom, whether from drawn-out torture or from sudden attack, was a constant in the newcomers' lives, but it was a risk they accepted willingly enough. Religion—the intense, devotional religion of the Catholic Counter-reformation—was in the very air the colonists breathed.

Jeanne Le Ber was a product of this time and this place. She was not a martyr like Father Jean de Brébeuf, nor even like Big Jean Boudart, a farmer struck down outside his house while trying to save his wife from Iroquois raiders. But give up her life she did, in a way that seems utterly foreign today.

The defining moment came in the early evening of August 5, 1695, a Friday. Montreal was then a town of perhaps 1,000 inhabitants, and many of them crowded along the street as the strange scene unfolded. François Dollier de Casson, superior of the colony's Sulpicians and seigneur of the island, led a small, solemn procession of clergy out from

Marguerite Bourgeoys, founder of the
Congrégation de Notre Dame teaching order.
(Plaster bust by Massard, 1852, collection of the Congrégation
de Notre Dame Centre Marguerite Bourgeoys.)

Notre Dame Church in Place d'Armes. They made their way down to Rue Saint-Paul and the two-storey house of Jacques Le Ber, a rich merchant.

Le Ber emerged from his house with his thirty-three-year-old daughter, Jeanne. Despite the family's wealth, she was dressed with unadorned simplicity in a plain woollen gown. A perceptive eye might have sensed how the calm of her face was at odds with the hints of distress in her father's.

Now the procession moved on, this time to the new chapel of the Congrégation de Notre Dame, the teaching order founded by the saintly Marguerite Bourgeoys. As they approached, the knowledge of what was about to happen proved too much for the old man. Sobbing, Jacques Le Ber broke away and rushed back to his house.

The procession entered the chapel. With the clergy and the sisters of the congregation looking on, as well as some ordinary folk whose curiosity had brought them inside, Jeanne sank to her knees. Dollier spoke briefly about the momentous step the young woman was about to take. Then he conducted her to an apartment behind the altar, and there she immediately locked herself in. As one of the priests intoned that evening, "You are dead, and enshrouded in your solitude as in a tomb. The dead do not speak, nor are they spoken to."

Jeanne Le Ber had turned her back on the world, the better to face God. There was nothing sudden or frivolous in her decision. As befits so profound an act of renunciation, she had been preparing for it for most of her life.

She was born in Montreal in 1662, and as a little girl was unusually introspective. She would often visit her godmother, Jeanne Mance, soaking up the pious atmosphere of the Hôtel-Dieu, the hospital that Mance had organized in the heroic days of Montreal's founding. In her early teens, she boarded with the Ursulines in Quebec City and then, at the age of fifteen, returned to her parents' home.

Once back in Montreal, she came under the wing of Marguerite Bourgeoys, and grew particularly attached to one of the sisters of the Congrégation de Notre Dame, a young woman about her own age. Her sudden death in 1679 deeply affected Jeanne, making plainer still her sense of religious vocation.

Perhaps her spiritual adviser, Abbé François Seguenot, had seen other cases of teenage enthusiasm lead to grief. In any case, he urged caution—that Jeanne should go into seclusion in a room in her parents' house, but just for five years. Only then might a further, perhaps irrevocable step be taken.

In her new life of austerity, Jeanne Le Ber wore a scratchy under-garment, and her shoes were made from corn husks. Sometimes, she would flog herself. She declined to visit her mother when the older woman lay dying just a few steps away, and later refused to take on the management of her widowed father's house, even though she was his only daughter. She emerged from her cell only to attend mass in the chapel of the Hôtel-Dieu, just along Rue Saint-Paul at Saint-Sulpice. So ostentatious was her piety—for example, she would kiss the floor at the elevation of the Host—that she began to draw attention to herself, the very thing a recluse might wish to avoid. Abbé Seguenot advised her to attend only the early mass each day, when fewer people were about.

Yet, something of Jeanne's old life lingered on into her new one. She was too frail, she said, to mortify herself by giving up meat, which other zealots habitually did. She insisted on a personal attendant, her cousin Anna Barroy, who did chores for her and went with her to mass. Far from getting rid of the wealth devolved on her by her father, she engaged in several business matters. And though the topics of conversation were generally religious, she did receive visitors from time to time.

The ambiguities continued when, her five-year trial completed, Jeanne took a formal vow of life-long seclusion, chastity and poverty. For example, she kept her money and chose to stay on in the house of her merchant father, which would have been a bustling place, rather than move to a more cloistered religious foundation.

Nonetheless, her vocation was genuine, a vocation in which the wealth she had retained would play an important part. The Congrégation de Notre Dame, which she so admired, then owned property below Rue Notre-Dame, where Boulevard Saint-Laurent now approaches the waterfront. When Jeanne learned that the sisters wanted to build a chapel there, she offered to put up a substantial part of the cost as well as provide them with an annual income of seventy-five *livres*.

But her generosity came with conditions. She would join the congregation, but instead of living communally with the other sisters she would remain immured in seclusion. The congregation would have to provide her with food, clothing, fuel and someone to step in should her cousin Anna not be on hand. They would pray for her daily.

The oddest condition by far described where Jeanne would live. The new chapel would include a bizarre, three-room apartment built directly behind the altar. Each room would be about ten feet square, and instead of being attached to one another in the normal way on one floor, the rooms would be stacked vertically.

The ground-floor room would have two doors, one leading outside to the sisters' garden, the other to the chapel itself. This second door would have a grille through which Jeanne could see the altar, receive communion and make her confession. Her bedchamber was above, with the bed at the wall nearest the chapel. Only the thinnest of partitions separated the tabernacle from her head while she slept. The topmost

Marguerite Bourgeoys ordered construction of the Maison Saint-Gabriel in Point St. Charles in 1698 to replace an earlier structure that burned down. The new building was first used as a school, and is still standing. (Watercolour by Georges Delfosse.)

room was where she would occupy herself with needlework.

This was the living sepulchre to which Dollier de Casson conducted her that August evening in 1695. For hours each day thereafter, Jeanne would pray or meditate. For just as long at night, when the other sisters were asleep, she would prostrate herself in front of the deserted chapel's altar. She also occupied herself not only with knitting clothes for the poor but with making altar cloths, chasubles, copes and other sacerdotal pieces. A surplice with an exquisite, brightly coloured floral design is preserved to this day at the congregation's Maison Saint-Gabriel in Point St. Charles, while other examples of her work are at Notre Dame Basilica.

And so the years passed. Her fame grew. Occasionally, visitors would ask to speak to her, and very occasionally one might be allowed to do so. The slightly ambiguous nature of her seclusion was persisting—and would do so as dramatically as ever in the summer of 1711.

The War of the Spanish Succession had embroiled England and France for almost a decade; a climax, at least for their respective North American colonies, was at hand. An English armada, the mightiest fleet this side of the Atlantic had ever seen, was to sail for the St. Lawrence from Boston under the command of Sir Hovenden Walker. Meanwhile, an army of 2,300 men led by Colonel Francis Nicholson would march along Lake Champlain and down the Richelieu River toward Montreal.

Near-panic gripped the town. With but a handful of soldiers to protect them, Montrealers turned to God. They crowded the churches and confessionals. They paraded penitentially through the streets, some in bare feet, others with nooses about their necks. Women vowed to give up lace, ribbons and other fripperies.

Montrealers also turned to Jeanne Le Ber and her aura of godliness. She was not so removed from the world that she was indifferent to the crisis. When approached to write a prayer for Montreal's salvation, she agreed. It was posted, of all places, on a barn owned by the Congrégation de Notre Dame:

"Our enemies put all their confidence in their arms, but we put ours in the name of the Queen of Angels, whom we invoke. She is terrible like an army ranged in battle. It is under her protection that we hope to vanquish our enemies."

Nonetheless, Montreal's situation was dire. Its rickety walls might withstand musket fire but certainly not English artillery. Its few soldiers had been sent off to bolster Quebec City's defences. Nevertheless, Charles Le Moyne de Longueuil, the local commander, assembled all the able-bodied men he could find. He also prevailed on Jeanne Le Ber, who was his cousin, to embroider a banner they would follow into battle. The banner, we are told, bore the prayer Jeanne had written.

There is a hint of another Jeanne here, Jeanne d'Arc, the mystic credited with saving France almost three centuries before. That earlier Jeanne was no recluse. She led French soldiers into the thick of the fighting, and had with her a banner bearing the lily of France, an image of Christ and the words *Jesus, Mary.*

Such boldness was not for Jeanne Le Ber, but her banner did have its own part to play. At a service of dedication in Notre Dame Church, François Vachon de Belmont, Dollier's successor as the Sulpicians' superior, blessed it and gravely gave it into Le Moyne's care. The tiny band with Le Moyne at its head set off to meet Nicholson's invaders, and Le Moyne carried the banner himself.

What followed, for those who believe in miracles, was just that—a miracle. While Jeanne Le Ber's banner slowly advanced on the English army, fog beset the enemy fleet as it entered the St. Lawrence. Seven ships drove onto rocks west of Sept-Isles. Hundreds of soldiers drowned; bodies and equipment were strewn along the shoreline or sank without

Jeanne Le Ber, 1662-1714, remains one of Montreal's most enigmatic figures. (Plaster bust by T. Carlo Petrucci Ltée, 1930, collection of Les Recluses Missionaires.)

a trace. Admiral Walker, choosing to see a merciful Providence intervening to preserve the survivors from "freezing, starvation and cannibalism," ordered the remaining ships back to Boston.

The English invaders advancing on Montreal by land were biding their time near Lake Champlain, waiting for the sea-borne assault to begin. When, instead, the news of the shipwrecks reached them, Nicholson was so angered he tore off his wig and stamped it into the ground. In disgust, he ordered his men to go home. Montreal was spared.

Jeanne Le Ber would live in a growing air of sanctity for another three years. Then, in September 1714, she fell ill. Congestion gripped her chest. She coughed constantly, and begged forgiveness for disturbing the devotions of those in the chapel just beyond her cell. Knowing the end was upon her, she gave the Congrégation de Notre Dame 18,000 *livres* and her furniture. She died on October 3 and two days later was laid in a genuine tomb beneath the congregation's chapel. Beside her was her father, who had died eight years before.

Britain finally got what it had long coveted when Quebec City fell in 1759, followed by Montreal a year later. The conquerors brought in their train the Protestant religion and the English language, and while neither was to be forced on the Catholic and French-speaking Canadians, the colony's new administrators weren't about to object to any conversions, religious or linguistic, that might occur. It was to nudge this process along that Rev. David Chabrand Delisle arrived in Montreal in 1766.

Delisle was not a zealot cut from the same cloth as Jeanne Le Ber, but he certainly was an oddity. He was born in the Protestant stronghold of Anduze, a town in the south of France once known as the Geneva of the Cevennes. By his teens he was studying divinity but, for reasons that are not clear, he did not see a future for himself as a pastor in his native country. He made his way to London, where he was ordained a priest of the Church of England in late 1764. He was just a few days short of his twenty-fourth birthday.

He surely struggled in the London parish where he was first assigned, for he could barely speak English. In fact, he was never remotely to master the language. However, his mother tongue suited him to other purposes. He was sent to Montreal as chaplain to the British garrison, but with the understanding that its souls were not his only concern. For his annual salary of £115, he was also expected to reveal the Protestant faith to Montreal's French-speaking Catholics. Thus would they be recast as proper inhabitants of the British Empire.

It was a near-impossible task. Not only was the Catholic religion a rare anchor for Canadians in the shifting tides of the day. In addition, while Quebec's clergy were willing enough to accommodate themselves to the new reality that the English-speaking Protestants among them represented, they remained deeply suspicious of the French Huguenot tradition from which Delisle sprang. In frustration, Delisle let it be known that he thought the Canadians were "the most ignorant and bigoted people in the world, and the most devoted to the priests, especially to the Jesuits." By 1771, he had won just two converts.

He was more successful on other fronts. In 1768, he was authorized to preach to Protestant civilians as well as soldiers, which he had been doing unofficially since his arrival. He often visited outlying districts. He was especially active on behalf of the poor. In 1773, he helped to bring Montreal its first Protestant schoolmaster, John Pullman.

Delisle's shaky English was not a great problem in these early years, for the English and Scottish merchants at the heart of Montreal's small Protestant community were nearly all bilingual. Certainly it was not shaky enough to prevent his marriage to Margaret Henry, from her name presumably an anglophone, in 1768. German-speaking Hessians who for a time served in the Montreal garrison preferred hearing sermons in his fluent French rather than his bad English.

All this changed, however, in the wake of the American Revolution. Loyalist families began flooding into Montreal, and many were unwilling to make allowances for Delisle's often-impenetrable idiom. Clergymen among them, especially Rev. John Doty and Rev. John Stuart from upstate New York, were also irked by Delisle's occasional departures from normal Anglican practices.

That Montreal's Anglicans, led by Delisle, had not yet managed to build their own church was another reproach. Thanks to Catholic indulgence, they were able to use the chapel of the Hôtel-Dieu and then the Récollets' chapel, but only at limited times. It was a "great mortification." The city's Presbyterians were moving toward building their own church on Rue Saint-Gabriel—it would be ready in 1792—and even the Jews had a synagogue, Montreal's first, by 1777, but the Anglicans were stalled.

Letters complaining of the sad state of Montreal Anglicanism were sent off to London. Twice, Doty travelled there himself to protest. Eventually, the complaints reached the ear of Bishop Charles Inglis in Halifax. His diocese of Nova Scotia stretched from Bermuda through the Maritime colonies to Quebec. He decided to see for himself what was going on.

In June 1789 he stopped over in Quebec City before moving on to Montreal, reaching the eastern tip of the island on July 2. A delegation including Delisle met him as he stepped ashore, then escorted him to the city.

There he discovered that matters were more or less as Doty had described them: the sacraments were indifferently administered, the Anglicans' use of the Récollet chapel was a humiliation and Delisle, though "respectable ... well bred and sensible," was impossible as a preacher because of his "disgusting and injurious" English. At a Sunday service, "a large and decent congregation ... could scarcely understand Mr. Delisle."

The bishop immediately set about shaking up things. He celebrated confirmation for 200 people, most of whom were adults. It was the first time Anglican confirmation had ever been administered in Montreal. He poked through the former chapel of the Jesuits, which had become a kind of storehouse after the British banished the order from the colony following the conquest. The government had promised to hand it over to the Anglicans, but nothing official had yet been proclaimed.

Nor would the pressure to do something about Delisle go away. Inglis had to meet a delegation of unhappy Montrealers who begged him to appoint a suitable assistant to the Frenchman. They even offered to raise £100 to support this hoped-for saviour.

The bishop had much to ponder by the time he got back to Quebec City, but within a week he was able to send good news to Montreal. The governor, Lord Dorchester, had confirmed that the Jesuit chapel would be theirs and was even contributing £300 for necessary repairs. Rev. James Marmaduke Tunstall, thirty years Delisle's junior, would become his nominal assistant though would take over most of his duties. Delisle would be allowed to preach in French "at such times as shall be judged expedient," Inglis decreed, and even occasionally in English, "though not often." Delisle's chief task, a thankless one, would be to proselytize among the Catholics.

It was a sad fate for an essentially good man. Surely the Anglicans recognized this when they asked Delisle to give the dedicatory sermon when the Jesuit chapel reopened in December 1789 as Montreal's first Christ Church. There is pathos between the lines of his acceptance of their offer, not least because he must have asked someone else to render it into proper English:

"Sensible that I owe this distinguished favour more to your good offices with my superiors than to my own long services, I beg leave to return you my sincere thanks. ... When I consider the solemnity of the occasion and the expectations of the hearers, I feel that I am not equal to the task. But encouraged by the experience I have of your indulgence and ardently desirous to evince my deference to your injunctions, I hope with divine assistance to preach a dedicatory sermon on the Sunday you will be pleased to appoint."

The sermon was a kind of valedictory. Delisle was now almost sixty and within a couple of years his health began to fail. He died on June 28, 1794.

"He found the fruits of his appointment bitter," historian James H. Lambert writes, "since he tasted the aversion for him of the Canadians, the insulting indifference towards him of most of his own congregation and, finally, near abandonment by the Church of England."

Perhaps as he lay dying, Delisle was able to reflect that Marmaduke Tunstall was proving a disappointment to the Anglicans as well. Tunstall's behaviour was becoming erratic and in 1796 he was obliged to take six months' leave in England. Not long after his return, however, it was clear that his mental derangement had returned with him. His absences became longer and more frequent. He was dragged into a squalid court case. Finally, the energetic Jehoshaphat Mountain had to take over the duties of rector. Tunstall's removal from Christ Church at the end of 1800 was a formality, albeit a painful one.

Montreal's Presbyterians were no strangers to such upsets, either. Unlike David Chabrand Delisle, however, Rev. Henry Esson was able to triumph over his adversaries.

Esson come out from Scotland in 1817. Rev. James Somerville was the incumbent at the Rue Saint-Gabriel church, where the Palais de Justice now stands, but he was elderly and in poor health. Esson would be his assistant, and perhaps his successor.

The young minister was soon drawn into church politics. The Anglican Church was "established" in Canada; Esson tirelessly badgered the authorities in London to win the same recognition for Presbyterians, which would give them a share in vast land holdings here known as the clergy reserves. Yet he also fought against those among his fellow Presbyterians who wanted to loosen the ties binding them to the mother church in Scotland.

In 1822, Somerville was finally pensioned off and Esson duly took over his pulpit. Not long after, he invited a fellow Scot, Rev. Edward Black, to share some of the preaching. Little did he anticipate the grief this would cause him.

St. Gabriel Street Church was the scene of a farcical siege by angry
Presbyterians in 1831.

Many of those Presbyterians found a home in the newly-built St. Paul's
Church nearby.

(Both illustrations from *Hochelaga Depicta, or the Early History of Montreal*
by Newton Bosworth, 1839.)

Esson was a scholarly, cultivated man. His sermons reflected the breadth of his learning, and indeed sometimes left his congregation wondering what he was getting at. Black by contrast relied not so much on reason as on emotion. His sermons were blunt, fiery and evangelical. The two men even looked different. Esson was slim, even delicate, whereas the bear-like, broad-shouldered Black was marked by "Luther-like features."

Many in the congregation were impressed by Black, but all realized they could not afford to pay the salaries of both men, as well as Somerville's pension. The congregation slowly but relentlessly split into two factions.

The inevitable explosion came in the spring of 1831. Early one Sunday morning, a group of Black's supporters sneaked into the Rue Saint-Gabriel church and barricaded the door behind them. When the rest of the congregation showed up at the normal hour for worship, they found they could not get in. Nor could Henry Esson, precisely what the Black camp wanted.

Rather to the surprise of the occupiers, however, the Presbyterians out in the street didn't quietly leave, taking the well-groomed Esson with them. Instead, they charged. They beat at the doors and tried to force them in, only to be defeated by the locks and the stout shoulders inside.

For other Montrealers gathered at the scene, it was great entertainment. They were "enjoying this extraordinary spectacle as a great joke."

The farce continued throughout the day and into the evening. The besiegers thought they might starve out the Black gang, but sympathizers managed to pass in some food through an unguarded window.

By the following day, cooler heads began to prevail and the siege dissolved. But not the underlying dispute: it took arbitrators appointed by an extraordinary synod of Presbyterian clergy to resolve matters, in Esson's favour as it turned out. Black left to take over the newly built St. Paul's Church in Rue Sainte-Hélène.

The Esson-Black struggle was of little interest to anyone beyond Montreal's Presbyterians, just as the tribulations of David Chabrand Delisle didn't really mean much to anyone but Anglicans. The lurid saga of Maria Monk was something else. No matter what their religion, people throughout the city, and elsewhere in Canada and the United States, were caught up in it as detail after sordid detail emerged.

At the centre of the storm was Montreal's Hôtel-Dieu, the city's oldest hospital with its attached convent. (This wasn't the same place where Jeanne Le Ber had prayed a century and a half before, but a rather larger complex built on the site after a fire in 1734.)

In October of 1835, a New York newspaper, the *American Protestant Vindicator,* claimed the Hôtel-Dieu was far from an island of sanctity. Behind the seeming calm of its grey stone, the newspaper shouted, there was fornication between nuns and priests, there was torture and there was murder. And how could all this be known? Why, thanks to the courage of Maria Monk, a young nun who had somehow managed to escape from its horrors. Once free, she felt duty-bound to warn other young women who might be tempted to take the veil. She told her story to the *Protestant Vindicator*, which promised that a much fuller account would soon appear in book form. The 200 pages of this book were duly published in January 1836 and bore the melodramatic title *Awful Disclosures of Maria Monk.*

Her descriptions of the sexual shenanigans at the Hôtel-Dieu were by no means explicit, at least by the standards of today. But no reader, then or now, could be under any illusions. Here is how Maria, immediately after taking her final vows, finally understood what was expected of her:

"I must be informed that one of my great duties was to obey the priests in all things; and this I soon learnt, to my utter astonishment and horror, was to live in the practice of criminal intercourse with them. ... I was required to act like the most abandoned of beings."

Her initiation into this abandon was not long in coming:

"Nothing important occurred until late in the afternoon, when, as I was sitting in the community-room, Father Dufresne called me out, saying he wished to speak with me. I feared what was his intention; but I dared not disobey. In a private apartment, he treated me in a brutal manner; and, from two other priests, I afterwards received similar usage that evening. Father Dufresne afterwards appeared again, and I was compelled to remain in company with him until morning."

Far from being the servants of God, Maria claimed, the sisters of the Hôtel-Dieu were the concubines of the priests in the Sulpician seminary across the street. A secret tunnel allowed the priests to visit the convent discreetly. Infants born from their lust were hastily baptized and then strangled before being thrown into a lime pit in the convent's cellars. Those nuns foolish enough to resist the demands of the priests could be confined, tortured, perhaps even murdered themselves. Maria had seen it all with her own eyes: the pit, several newborns smothered, a young sister crushed to death by a priest and some older nuns jumping up and down on her pinioned form.

In time, Maria found she was pregnant. Lest her baby suffer the fate of the other newborns, she escaped and made her way to New York. Kind people sheltered her and encouraged her to tell her story. The result was the *Awful Disclosures*.

Perhaps there were a few bigots in Montreal who took this tale of iniquity as gospel. Overwhelmingly, however, the instant reaction of most people in the city was horror mixed with fury. They were angry not because such abominations were apparently going on, but because someone could have been so malicious as to suggest they were. There could scarcely have been a more venerated institution in the city than the Hôtel-Dieu. The selfless behaviour of its nuns when cholera had recently afflicted the city—caring for the sick, giving solace to the bereaved—was merely the latest demonstration of their worth.

Protestants as well as Catholics, English Montrealers as well as French, were outraged. Such unanimity was all the more remarkable given the communal tensions that would erupt into armed rebellion less than two years later. For example, look at what the *Montreal Herald* had to say on October 20, just a few days after the *Protestant Vindicator*'s story and months before the appearance of the *Awful Disclosures*.

"We will not disgrace our columns nor disgust our readers by copying the false, the abominably false article," the *Herald* wrote. "Though of a different religious persuasion from the priests and nuns, we have had too many opportunities of witnessing their unwearied assiduity and watchfulness and Christian charity during two seasons of pestilence, and can bear witness to the hitherto unimpeached and unimpeachable rectitude of their conduct to be in the slightest degree swayed in our opinion by a newspaper slander. ...

"We do not pretend to be defenders of the Roman Catholic religion or of any of its particular institutions. We are Protestants and glory in being so, but we will not so far forget the precepts of Our Divine Master as to connive at traducing the character of individuals who are exemplary members of society."

The truth began to emerge just a few days later. Maria Monk's real-life story was squalid, too, as squalid in its own way as the false life she had invented for herself.

She was born in 1816 in Saint-Jean-sur-Richelieu, the daughter of respectable Scots, and soon proved herself a difficult child. When she was seven, she jammed a pencil into her ear, evidently touching her brain, and thereafter her behaviour became more and more erratic. In her teens, she slipped into drink and prostitution. Finally, in November 1834, her mother committed her to Montreal's Magdalen Asylum. It was a refuge for prostitutes, and it was the only Catholic institution she would ever inhabit.

Maria was eighteen, pregnant and quite uninterested in the asylum's efforts to reform her. There's even a suggestion she tried to persist in her old life from behind its walls. The matron later testified that one day Maria "held conversation with a man who had reached the yard of the Asylum by scaling the enclosures." Conversation, of course, might mean mere chat, or it might carry the older meaning of sexual intimacy. In March, she was thrown out—just about the time she gave birth.

She ran off to New York with a man named William Hoyte. He was a Protestant minister and ferociously anti-Catholic. There's evidence to suggest he might also have been the man who scaled the asylum's walls, perhaps even the father of her child. In New York, they hooked up with some other like-minded Protestants, so-called nativists who were convinced that the New World was being swamped by Catholic immigrants from the Old. This no-popery-here cabal began to concoct the *Awful Disclosures*. Hoyte and his friends did the actual writing, with the perfervid imagination of Maria providing local Montreal colour.

That few people in Montreal gave any credence to the *Awful Disclosures* was small comfort to Jean-Jacques Lartigue. At first, Montreal's Catholic bishop was inclined to do nothing, preferring not to dignify Maria's claims with a response. Evidence that she had made it all up was mounting; even Rev. W.C. Brownlee, editor of the *Protestant Vindicator,* was backing away from what he had printed. Still, the book continued to sell—26,000 copies by July 1836. Bishop Lartigue concluded he could stand idle no longer, especially when he learned that Colonel William L. Stone was coming to Montreal to investigate Maria's charges.

Stone was a well-known author and the editor of the *New York Commercial Advertiser.* He was a Protestant with nativist sympathies, but he also had a reputation for fair-mindedness. When he asked for permission to tour the Hôtel-Dieu, Lartigue consented. He knew the convent had nothing to hide; perhaps the testimony of an eminent American Protestant that this was so would finally drive a stake through the heart of Maria's story.

Stone arrived in Montreal in October 1836. Twice he visited the Hôtel-Dieu. With a copy of the *Awful Disclosures* in hand, he searched every room, every closet, every corridor, from the attics down to—yes— the cellars. He could find no secret tunnel, no lime pit. He interviewed the sisters. He could find no evidence of a nun named Jane Ray, whom Maria had claimed as an ally, much less any memory of a nun named Maria Monk.

Together with G.W. Perkins, minister of the American Presbyterian Church in Montreal, Stone was even able to interview Maria herself. Time and again, her descriptions of the Hôtel-Dieu's layout contradicted what Stone had just seen with his own eyes.

Then, rather like magic, Maria's partisans produced another supposed refugee from the Hôtel-Dieu called Sister St. Francis Patrick. She and Maria appeared together at a public meeting, and gave every appearance of being long-lost friends. But their effusions were all show business. This second woman was a lost soul named Frances Partridge, and she was no more credible than Maria. The nunnery of her imaginings differed both from Maria's and from what Stone now knew to be true.

Stone quickly brought out a book titled *Maria Monk's Show-up!!!* —complete with exclamation marks—in which the story was denounced as humbug. With Stone's testimony, the tide began to turn in earnest against Maria. She, or rather Hoyte and company, brought out new editions with even more awful disclosures. For example, Nuns' Island, close to Montreal's harbour, was where nuns from all over Canada and the United States went to have their illegitimate babies. A few benighted creatures, standing on the wilder shores of anti-Catholic bigotry, continued to take it all in, but most people were fed up.

By then, Maria herself seems to have had enough, too. Perhaps she began to realize how Hoyte was using her. Perhaps her fragile mind was moving on to some wholly new parallel universe. She left Hoyte, and for a time shared the bed of one of his clerical fellow-authors. She had another child. She found a man who actually married her, but he soon decamped when her continuing antics overwhelmed him.

In 1849, in a New York brothel, she lifted the wallet of one of her clients. She was promptly arrested and, by now quite mad, was locked up in the Blackwell's Island prison. There, that summer, she died. Yet even today, as a quick Internet search will show, there are those who cling to her story of depravity at the Hôtel-Dieu. For them, Maria Monk will never die.

This was by no means the end of Catholic-baiting in Montreal. One of the city's most appalling outbursts of zealotry gone wild lay just a few years off.

Alessandro Gavazzi was an Italian monk who, in the 1840s, took up liberal politics. He became persuaded that the Catholic Church was corrupt, yet maintained that his increasingly virulent attacks on the papacy were prompted not by malice but by a desire to reform the institution. To traditional Catholics, it was all lies and blasphemy; to his supporters, he was Alessandro the Great.

In June of 1853 Gavazzi, by then unfrocked, was in Canada and the United States preaching his incendiary message. In a Protestant church in Quebec City, Catholic demonstrators tried to shout him down. Bibles were thrown at him. Clubs appeared, and the mob began to press toward the pulpit. Gavazzi tried to beat them off with a chair, but was pulled from his perch and thrown fifteen feet to the floor of the church. His partisans were lucky to whisk him away.

More of the same was feared when he moved on—with a visibly battered face—to Montreal on June 9. He spoke that evening in Zion Congregational Church on Beaver Hall Hill and, sure enough, there was another uproar. Enraged protesters, mainly Irish Catholics, tried breaking into the church to disrupt the lecture but were turned back by

Soldiers fire as Irish Catholics grapple with supporters of Alessandro Gavazzi in front of Zion Congregational Church, Beaver Hall Hill. The defrocked monk had been lecturing there against the supposed evils of Catholicism.
(Illustration by Peter Le Sueur, 1853.)

Gavazzi's equally determined supporters.

Extra police were on hand because precisely this sort of ruckus was expected, but they were helpless to restore order. The swirling tumult moved down the hill toward the Haymarket, today's Victoria Square.

Mayor Charles Wilson had also arranged for a squad of about 100 men from a Scottish regiment, the Cameronians, to be held in reserve inside the fire hall by the square. Seeing the police in disarray, Wilson grew desperate. He ordered the officers to deploy their men in two lines across Beaver Hall Hill, one facing downhill into the square itself and the other facing up toward the church.

Perhaps the arrival of the soldiers cooled some tempers; certainly the fighting in the Haymarket seemed to be waning. Then several pistol shots were heard. Wilson's desperation began to verge on panic. He read the Riot Act, but such was the noise all about him that he could scarcely be heard.

What happened next remains murky. No one would admit it then, and no one knows to this day, who gave the order to fire. But fire the soldiers did: down into the square and, a minute later, up toward the church where what remained of Gavazzi's audience, the lecture concluded, were emerging into the street. When it was over, fifteen people lay dead—trampled, clubbed or shot—and another twenty-five were injured.

It took rather longer for the anger to subside. There was an official inquiry several weeks later, but suspicions persisted when its findings were suppressed. On several occasions, Cameronians unwise enough to walk the streets alone were attacked. Someone sneaked into the council chambers and cut away the head from Mayor Wilson's portrait.

Gavazzi didn't wait around to see any of this. His friends hustled him straight from Zion Church to the St. Lawrence Hall, the hotel on St. James Street where he was staying (and where more Cameronians were posted to guard him). Later that night, two Protestant ministers smuggled him down to the waterfront and onto a ferry to the South Shore. He was soon on his way to New York.

Gavazzi's presence in Montreal, though devastating, was mercifully brief. Rev. Charles Chiniquy, his near-exact contemporary, would be a part of the city's life for more than half a century. A decade before Montrealers had ever heard of Gavazzi, Chiniquy was launched on an anti-booze crusade that would help make him the best-known Catholic priest not just in Montreal but throughout French Canada.

Like Gavazzi, Chiniquy was born in 1809. The Kamouraska native was ordained in 1833 and five years later was given the important parish of Beauport, near Quebec City. There, wherever his eyes fell, he saw drunkenness; there, he found the first great cause of his life. Commanding as an orator despite his slight build, he campaigned relentlessly against the evils of drink. He founded a temperance society and within a year some 2,000 people had taken the pledge. His renown grew. He made "a great sensation" in October 1841 when he came to Montreal and preached to thousands in Notre Dame Church.

His style was over the top. He would start a sermon softly, but soon would seem almost possessed by his message. Sometimes shouting, sometimes sobbing, he would inveigh against drink and how it could ravage a drinker's body and drinkers' families. The detail was graphic, often tasteless. It was shamelessly theatrical, often horrifying and astonishingly effective.

Yet in campaigning against this all-too-common weakness, Chiniquy was prey to a weakness of his own. Plainly put, the young priest was a lecher.

He seems to have started young. At the age of fifteen, he was banished from the home of an uncle, where he had been living since his father's death three years before. Chiniquy would always say it was because of a misunderstanding. But years later, a grandson of the uncle, Bishop Henri Têtu, testified otherwise. The teenaged Chiniquy, Têtu suggested in his memoirs, had been caught trying to seduce a young female cousin.

The pattern—if pattern it was—reappeared in Beauport. Despite his fast-growing fame as a temperance crusader, Chiniquy was suddenly dispatched back to darkest Kamouraska as a mere assistant curé. Archbishop Joseph Signay of Quebec, hitherto his patron, gave no reason, but rumours persisted that—shall we say—an incident between Chiniquy and his housekeeper was his undoing.

Nonetheless, he continued to campaign against booze, and for a time parishes near and far loved it. In one Lower South Shore parish alone, 1,300 people promised to forswear drink. He wrote a book aimed at young people who might be tempted. But in October 1846, as suddenly as he was hustled out of Beauport, he announced he was leaving Kamouraska to join the Missionary Oblates of Mary Immaculate in Longueuil, across the St. Lawrence from Montreal.

The Oblates were famous for preaching temperance, and Chiniquy claimed he was disgusted by the excesses of the regular clergy. In truth, it was a familiar excess of his own. It seems his wandering eye had been caught by the charms of a woman in Saint-Pascal, four miles from Kamouraska. He made his move; she resisted. He kept trying, and finally she agreed to a rendezvous. When he arrived, however, Chiniquy found waiting for him not an amorous housewife but Saint-Pascal's angry priest.

It was farcical, but of course scandalous. No longer could a blind eye be turned to similar incidents at three other parishes. No longer could anyone ignore how a growing number of parents were sending their youngsters elsewhere for confession, lest they fall prey to "baneful contact" with Chiniquy.

Leaving Kamouraska to become an Oblate novice was part of the necessary cover-up. Nonetheless, Chiniquy didn't react well to this respite. Restless as ever, he bridled under the Oblates' rules of obedience and, once too often, he criticized the order's leadership. By the fall of 1847, he was out.

But of course not down: Bishop Ignace Bourget of Montreal, who had invited him to preach at Notre Dame in 1841, now asked him to resume the fight against drink in the city.

This new crusade, which lasted for more than three years, proved one of Chiniquy's greatest triumphs. A rally at Bonsecours Market in October 1848 drew 5,000 people, including Bourget and Mayor Joseph Bourret. By the end of the year, it was said he had converted 60,000 people to abstinence. Thousands more flocked to his standard the following spring. His portrait, sold in bookstores, was hung with reverence in countless homes. Bourget presented him with a gold crucifix the bishop had brought back from Rome. In 1850, the government of the Province of Canada awarded him £500 in recognition of his good works.

The vaulting popularity of Chiniquy's crusade, the way it might expose Chiniquy to pride, that most deadly of sins, began to make Bourget uneasy. He was also bothered by what he had come to know of Chiniquy's character. When the priest was invited early in 1851 to preach in the isolated French-Canadian communities of St. Anne and Bourbonnais, south of Chicago, Bourget sent him off with a three-part warning.

"Take strict precautions in your relations with persons of the opposite sex," Bourget wrote. "Avoid carefully all that might savour of ostentation, and the desire to attract attention; simplicity is so beautiful and lovable a virtue. Pay to the priests of the country the honour due to their ministry; the glory of God is the best recompense of an apostolic man."

Bourget was right on the money with his apprehensions. Chiniquy, on his way to Chicago, stopped over in Detroit where he began to pay "offensive attentions to the daughter of a respectable family." He hastily resumed his journey when he learned the local bishop was aware of his knavery and was about to intervene.

Then, upon his return to Montreal, there was more of the same. A young woman accused him of improper behaviour. Chiniquy tried claiming it was the other way around. She had tried to entice him into sin, he said, and he had refused. She had complained to the bishop out of spite, nothing else.

But by then Bourget had too much experience of Chiniquy's slipperiness to be taken in. "We had had proof of M. Chiniquy's guilt for some time," Bourget wrote, obviously referring to his previous indiscretions, "when a certain girl came to give evidence against him, testifying that she would feel repugnance to be confronted by him." This was the last straw. Once again, he had to go. Providentially for Bourget, a more trusting bishop, James Van de Velde of Chicago, invited Chiniquy to move to St. Anne permanently.

Once established in Illinois, Chiniquy continued to ruffle feathers. While by and large his new parishioners adored him, it was different for his fellow clergy. Not only did he continue to unsettle Bourget, this time by encouraging emigration from Montreal to the United States. In addition, Van de Velde and then his two successors as bishop of Chicago agonized over reports of the turbulence that continued to swirl about the Canadian priest.

He was flamboyant. There were hints of heresy in his sermons. Other —and it must be said less energetic—priests in the diocese complained. He was sued for slander (and was defended by a gangly young lawyer from Springfield, Illinois, named Abraham Lincoln). He wanted the chapel in Bourbonnais rebuilt in stone, and quarrelled with Van de Velde when the bishop insisted on less expensive wood. When the half-finished structure mysteriously burned down one night, whispers immediately began that Chiniquy himself was responsible.

And sure enough, to top it all there was the old problem of lust. Not only was he accused of visiting "women of ill repute" but he even tried to have his way with the wife of St. Anne's sexton, blithely assuring her that priests really weren't barred from sexual relations.

Anthony O'Regan, who succeeded Van de Velde in 1854, was

determined to run a tighter ecclesiastical ship. After two years of trying to bring Chiniquy to heel, he finally suspended him from his duties. When Chiniquy failed to submit with sufficient humility, O'Regan excommunicated him outright. Undaunted, the unruly priest continued to preach and to administer the sacraments as if not a thing had changed.

The drawn-out tussle helped drive O'Regan out of the diocese and into an early retirement. It was left to his steely successor, John Duggan, to travel to St. Anne and confirm the excommunication on the spot.

That finally did it. Shortly afterward, Chiniquy formally defected to Protestantism, taking the better part of his congregation at St. Anne with him.

Thus began the second great cause of his life. Once, his enemy was alcohol. Now it was the Roman Catholic Church. Peaceful co-existence was not for him. He was determined to bring the church low, and wouldn't shrink from the most outrageous lies if they were what it took.

Year after year, in fiery speeches, magazine articles and books, he condemned the church for its supposed paganism. Catholics worshiped the Virgin Mary as a goddess. The pope was directing a vast conspiracy to flood the United States with Catholic immigrants and make the country a Catholic one. The U.S. Civil War and the assassination of Lincoln, his one-time lawyer, were Catholic plots.

In 1864, Chiniquy married his housekeeper and soon they had three children. Perhaps marriage was all it took, for the lechery that had so tarnished his life as a Catholic priest now seemed to abate. Nonetheless, sex continued to preoccupy him.

Witness his attacks on Catholic confession. In his 1875 book *Le prête, la femme et le confessional,* he offered salacious examples of priests who were so aroused by the racy confessions of women that they soon fell into sin themselves. Yet confession could work the other way round, too. By questioning children about lewdness and other failings, Chiniquy fulminated, a priest in fact put sinful ideas into their heads.

In an ugly way, he knew what he was talking about, as all the young women he'd approached could testify, as well as the Kamouraska parents who had been so anxious to shield their children from him.

Nor did he shrink from the vulgarity that so often marked his tirades against alcohol. During a service in Montreal in 1875, he contemptuously trampled some communion wafers underfoot. Not just Catholics but many Protestants were offended.

In 1873, the Presbyterian Church in Canada put him in charge of its mission to convert Catholics. He toured tirelessly, stirring up controversy, even violence, wherever he went. In Quebec City in 1884, stones began to crash through the window of the church where he was preaching. Afterward, angry Catholics chased his carriage to the railway station where he escaped their wrath by hiding in a trunk. The mob tore his carriage apart instead.

He also inspired anger among Protestants, though of course it was directed not at him but at Catholics. The same sort of bigots who swallowed what Maria Monk had to tell them were equally persuaded by Chiniquy. His 1885 memoir *Cinquante ans dans l'Église de Rome* was a huge success. It was translated into many languages, and Catholic bishops around the world were often in touch with their Quebec colleagues seeking advice on how to counter the threat.

He remained true to his convictions—that is, to his convictions since 1858—until the end. As he lay dying in January 1899, Chiniquy received a letter from Montreal's Archbishop Paul Bruchési, urging him to consider returning to Rome. He declined, though with surprising civility, to meet the prelate. Instead, he put the final touches on a religious testament in which he returned to his violent condemnation of the church. It was published a week after his death.

Just before he died, two nuns managed to sneak into his house, thinking they might succeed where Bruchési had failed. They were discovered and, politely but firmly, were shown the door. They should have known they had no chance.

In actual conversions, Chiniquy was less successful than his undeniable fame would suggest. No more than a few thousand Catholics in Quebec are thought to have grasped his standard, and far fewer in the United States.

One of his rare triumphs had come late in 1868, when he preached for three days at the Indian settlement of Oka, also known as Kanesatake, a little west of Montreal on the Ottawa River. The 400 or so Mohawks living there were so impressed by his message that they appealed to the Methodists to send them a missionary. Rev. Xavier Rivet duly arrived, and before long most of Oka's Mohawks abandoned the Catholic Church to become Wesleyan Methodists.

Yet it wasn't simply religious conviction that was at issue. More than embracing Methodism, they were protesting against Catholicism, or rather the betrayal it had come to represent. Lying behind their conversion was a history of disappointment, even anger, that has continued to this day, erupting most explosively in the Oka crisis of 1990.

In 1721, the Sulpicians established a mission at Oka on a seigneury they had acquired several years before by royal authority. The mission would provide a haven for Catholic Mohawks and Algonkians who, so long as they lived on Montreal Island, were exposed to liquor traders and other evils. Yet the precise nature of the land grant was in dispute from the outset. Did the land fundamentally belong to the Indians, being held in trust for them by the Sulpicians? Or was it owned by the Sulpicians outright?

The Indians rejected the Sulpicians' claim to ownership on many occasions. In 1851, a Methodist minister from Ontario, a Mississauga Ojibwa named Peter Jones, capitalized on Oka's unrest and nearly persuaded several Mohawks to renounce the Catholic faith. Not for nothing was he known by the Mohawk name Desagondensta ("he stands people on their feet").

The immediate Sulpician response to Desagondensta was to engineer the excommunication of fifteen Oka dissidents. For the longer term, they began to groom a promising young Mohawk named Joseph Onasakenrat to be their bulwark-in-chief against further Protestant assaults. Raised as a Catholic, the fifteen-year-old Onasakenrat was sent to the Sulpicians' Petit Séminaire in Montreal. He did well in his studies, and when he returned to Oka three years later he was made secretary to the Sulpician pastor there, Father Antoine Mercier.

But Onasakenrat was not the pliant Mohawk his patrons thought he was. In 1868, he was elected chief of the Oka band. Shortly afterward, he sent a petition to the governor general, Viscount Monck, renewing the Indian claim to the land held by the Sulpicians. The anger in the document was plain. The priests were "the pretended successors of St. Peter." They lived in sumptuous comfort while the Indians languished in poverty and misery. No wonder they were so open to Chiniquy a few months later.

Onasakenrat stepped up his campaign early the following year. On February 18, 1869, he chopped down a giant elm tree, a calculated, highly visible defiance of the Sulpicians' exclusive right to Oka's timber. A week later, with forty other Mohawks, he marched on the Sulpicians' rectory and demanded they leave the seigneury immediately.

Indignant, the Sulpicians got a warrant for Onasakenrat's arrest. Montreal police took him and three others in hand on March 4. But he was soon released, more determined than ever to carry on.

In late 1869, there was a petition to the new governor general, Lord Lisgar. A kind of guerrilla war broke out, in which the Indians chopped down trees and destroyed Sulpician fences. Often the police were called and more Indians arrested. The Sulpicians began selling lots to white newcomers, the beginnings of today's town of Oka. In 1875, the priests pulled down the Indians' new Methodist church, claiming they had no right to erect it in the first place.

A climax came on June 15, 1877, when the 150-year-old Sulpician church burned to the ground. The priests were certain it was arson, especially when one of them saw Onasakenrat and his father hanging around the blaze. Warrants for the arrest of the two, plus about a dozen other Indians, were issued.

Some prominent Montrealers were only too pleased to provide legal and financial help to the defendants, whom they saw as fellow English-speaking Protestants struggling against Catholic oppression. Some organized a campaign to collect provisions "for these poor people ... in deep want, owing to late events." *The Gazette,* which eight years before decried Onasakenrat's tree-chopping as "Indian outrages," was now strongly sympathetic.

In reality, of course, the struggle was neither religious nor linguistic but cultural, between Indians (who only incidentally were Methodists and English-speaking) and whites (who happened to be Catholics and French-speaking). Four times the jury failed to reach a verdict. It took a fifth trial, in 1881, to find Onasakenrat and his companions not guilty.

Through it all, Onasakenrat found increasing comfort in Methodism. He translated the four gospels into the Iroquoian tongue and, in 1880, was ordained a Methodist minister. He began preaching among fellow Mohawks in Kahnawake, across the river from Montreal, and at Akwesasne, near Cornwall, Ontario. Perhaps worn out by more than a decade of confrontation, he began to urge an accommodation with the Sulpicians. When the priests offered to buy the Indians a tract of land between Lake Muskoka and Georgian Bay, and pay their moving expenses as well, Onasakenrat urged them to accept.

It was not what most of them wanted to hear. Late in 1881, fewer than 100 Mohawks agreed to the proposed move. Later, when the land proved much less suitable than they had been led to believe, many soon began drifting back to Oka.

But by then, Onasakenrat was no more. He died in some agony on February 7, 1881, the result, according to the coroner's inquest, of "debilitation of the heart and congestion of the lungs." Yet there were whisperings that his old antagonists, the Sulpicians, were in fact to blame. He had been invited to dine with them in Montreal, and shortly afterward fell ill. The reason, for many Mohawks, was clear: the ever-vindictive priests had deliberately poisoned him.

In 1910, the Supreme Court finally confirmed the priests' ownership of the Oka seigneury. But instead of trying to consolidate their position, the Sulpicians were now free to sell off the property in earnest. By 1936, a little more than two centuries after they had arrived, they were gone. Indian anger remained, to blaze up so fiercely—and fatally—in 1990 when the town of Oka began extending a golf course adjacent to the old Mohawk cemetery. Joseph Onasakenrat's grave was an unquiet one.

However odd Jeanne Le Ber and David Chabrand Delisle might seem to us today, there is no reason to doubt the sincerity of their religious vocations. Poor, demented Maria Monk surely believed, to the extent permitted by her fragile mental health, in what was written in her name. Even Charles Chiniquy, for all his cynical opportunism, was a man of genuine if misguided conviction, as, indeed, was Alessandro Gavazzi.

Ignatius Timotheus Trebitsch is much harder to pin down. Zeal was undeniably a constant in his life, but not conviction. He changed his religious stripes as other men change their shirts. For him, it was important to believe not in this creed or that doctrine but simply to believe. He is a bizarre and fascinating figure. In weaker moments, we might even find it admirable how, time and again, he smoothly reinvented himself. But that is to be seduced by the man. Trebitsch was a con artist, in religion and much else besides.

He was born Ignácz Trebitsch into a bourgeois Jewish family in 1879. Nathan, his traditionally minded father, was a well-off merchant in the town of Paks, south of Budapest, and as Ignácz grew into his teens he found the atmosphere at home more and more stifling. He was precocious, showing a remarkable gift for languages, but restless. He played hooky from school. The bright lights of Budapest, where the family eventually moved, were hard for him to ignore.

Then the once-prosperous Nathan fell on hard times. There seemed no future for young Ignácz in the Hungarian capital, and so he took off. Besides, the police were interested in him—something about a stolen gold watch. He was just eighteen.

Drifting to London, he was taken in by an East End mission that aimed to bring Jews to Christianity. Perhaps it was a way of thumbing his nose at his father, but a seed was planted. By the time he got to Hamburg and a similar mission there, he was ready. On Christmas Day of 1899, under the guidance of the Irish Presbyterian Church, he became a Christian and less than two weeks later entered a seminary. Yet the signs of his spiritual inconstancy were plain. That seminary was Lutheran, not Presbyterian, and in any event he left after just four months.

For reasons that are now lost, he decided to try his luck in Montreal. He arrived in the summer of 1900 and, as he had in London, found shelter in yet another mission aimed at Jews. The mission, on Dorchester Street, was ostensibly non-denominational. But it was run by a Presbyterian, Rev. John McCarter, and Trebitsch accordingly decided he was a Presbyterian after all. McCarter for his part decided Trebitsch was little short of a gift from God. Within a few months, the smooth young man with the dapper moustache and wavy hair was McCarter's full-time assistant. The mission was impoverished and Trebitsch's salary was just a few hundred dollars a year, but it was his first job.

The great Jewish migration to Montreal was then getting underway. The number of Jews in the city had almost trebled to about 6,700 in the previous decade, and vastly more would cross the Atlantic as persecution increased, especially in eastern Europe. Overwhelmingly, they were desperately poor when they arrived in Montreal, knowing neither English nor French. They clustered in the streets and lanes around Dufferin Square, where Complexe Guy Favreau now stands.

The area was like a shtetl lifted straight from the Old Country, "throbbing with Jewish life" as Yiddish-language journalist Israel Medres once wrote. "The corner of St. Urbain and Dorchester was the very heart of the Jewish neighbourhood. Nearby was Dufferin Park, then a 'Jewish park' where Jewish immigrants went to breathe the fresh air, meet others from their old home towns, hear the latest news, look for work and read the newspapers."

From his base in McCarter's nearby mission, Trebitsch leapt right in. He disputed with Jews wherever he found them, even in their homes. In that polyglot neighbourhood, he seemed equally at ease in Hungarian, Yiddish and German. He even preached in English, though surely to uncertain effect. He passed out tracts and passages from the Bible in Yiddish, and managed to attract a few Jews to Bible classes back at the mission. Yet despite all his energy, he failed to win a single convert. Montreal's Jews overwhelmingly were Orthodox and devout or, in a few cases, socialist and sceptical. Either way, they were too tough for the young missionary.

A year later, a discouraged and exhausted McCarter had had enough. He told Trebitsch he was giving up the mission to which he had devoted himself for six years but would recommend him as his successor. Trebitsch saw his chance. He had no confidence the Presbyterian Church would be any more eager to subsidize the mission under his direction than it had been when McCarter ran it. But he also knew that the Anglicans, through the London Society for the Promotion of Christianity Among the Jews, wanted to be active in Montreal. And so began a courtship between Trebitsch and Rev. A.F. Burt, the society's organizing director for Canada. It was a whirlwind affair, and as each party wanted the other, the outcome was never really in doubt.

"Found splendidly qualified convert deeply spiritual seven languages shall I retain?" an excited Burt cabled the society's headquarters in London, and by the spring of 1902, everything was falling into place. The Presbyterians withdrew their interest, the well-heeled

Anglicans took over the mission and Trebitsch was the man in charge.

On August 4, the society set him up in a house on Rue de La Gauchetière a couple of blocks off the Main. There was room for the mission on the ground floor and living quarters for him and his new wife above.

Burt has vividly described Trebitsch as he evangelized in the street one day:

"All around us is a bedlam of gesticulating volubility. Rude jests, laughter, sneers, catcalls, and discordant interruptions are heard on the outskirts of the crowd, the nucleus of which is formed by us and two or three particular Jews, arguing together, with one another and with us, simultaneously.

"Hard thrusts, not always polite, are given by the listeners, which Mr. Trebitsch takes with the utmost good humour and returns with equal vigour. Very soon, the disputants begin to grow excited. They leave English and use several languages. ... Some turn away, visibly disgusted that the rest give any attention to the missionary; and others, more curious, take their places."

The new mission was formally opened October 16 with no less a figure than Archbishop William Bond present. But though it was an Anglican show that day, Rev. John Scrimger, soon to be principal of Montreal's Presbyterian College, was also among the speakers. "We owed a great debt of gratitude to the Jews," Scrimger said, "and there was no better way of repaying it than by lovingly, tenderly, gently, kindly, and in a Christian spirit carrying to them the message of our faith." Trebitsch, he said, was ideally qualified for this task.

Trebitsch himself also spoke, presenting "the claims of Christ to the Jews in attendance in their respective languages: Hebrew, Yiddish, German and Hungarian." But not everyone in the neighbourhood was so welcoming. Three days later, a crowd of agitated Jews began demonstrating outside the house. "The opening is a thorn in their sides," Trebitsch said. "I noticed at once their intention, and tried to prevent it by exceptionally kind words. They listened fairly attentively, although they disturbed my address."

A month later, Archbishop Bond confirmed him as an Anglican, and on December 21, in Christ Church Cathedral, he was made a deacon.

Bond, from the evangelical wing of the church, seemed especially fond of Trebitsch and, according to Trebitsch's wife, said "he would not be the least surprised to see him step into his shoes and become archbishop of Montreal."

It was his Montreal zenith, even if there is nothing to suggest he was any more a committed Anglican than he had been a Presbyterian, a Lutheran or a Jew. But then he made what his biographer Bernard Wasserstein calls "a fatal blunder." In January 1903, he threatened to leave the mission unless his pay was substantially increased, and in February he proposed that the Montreal mission declare its independence from London. Both notions went nowhere, whereupon Trebitsch turned his back on religion—temporarily, to be sure—and quit.

He was soon on a boat to England. The next four decades would see him increasingly flip in and out of delusion, all the while assuming a dizzying array of callings. He was an Anglican curate in rural England, a British MP and a censor for Britain's War Office in the First World War—none of which prevented him from spying for Germany (using La Gauchetière as his codename). He tried his hand at promoting oil wells. He was a sensationalist author and journalist. He was a leading conspirator in the 1920 Kapp putsch that tried to overthrow the German government, during which he caught the eye of a disaffected ex-corporal named Adolf Hitler. He plotted against the new Bolshevik regime in Russia. He was a fugitive from justice in Britain and the United States, and served time in prison for forgery.

He used a dizzying array of names as well: Trebitsch Lincoln, Patrick Keelan, Theodor Lakatos, Heinrich Lamprecht, Dr. Tibor Lehotzky, Thomas Langford, Vilmos Ludwig, and Anagarika Pukkasati, to list just some.

His most astonishing metamorphosis came well into his middle age, when he fell under the spell of the Orient. In 1927, *The Gazette* reported that one Ignatius Thibitsch Lincoln, "self-confessed spy, deportee, arch-intriguer and adventurer," had become chief political and financial adviser to the southern Chinese armies. For the moment he was in Berlin, he said, seeking a $20-million loan to underwrite a Chinese invasion of French Indo-China, Tibet, Afghanistan and Persia.

Spiritual chameleon as ever, he also had a new religion, this time

Tibetan-influenced Buddhism. In 1931, under the name Chao Kung, he was ordained a Buddhist monk in a monastery near Nanking. Two years later he set up a monastery for Westerners in Shanghai, with himself as abbot. He had better luck than in Montreal, attracting a dozen or more acolytes to his side.

Late in 1933, he took it into his head to try establishing a monastery in Switzerland. The following March, accompanied by four monks and six nuns, he sailed to Vancouver and boarded a train for the east coast. The journey took him through Montreal, where the party put up for several days at the Queen's Hotel. It was the first time Trebitsch had seen the city since his hasty departure more than thirty years before.

Trebitsch and his fellow Buddhists stood out, to say the least. "All have shaven heads and the colored dots at regular intervals on their crowns," the *Montreal Daily Herald* reported. "They wear black habits and a kind of artificial pigtail, as well as strings of beads."

In a long interview with the *Herald*, he said he was on his way to London seeking reinstatement as a British subject. "I was a liar once," he cheerfully admitted. "I have turned, and have become a man of truth." Alas, the British authorities were not convinced. When his ship docked in England, he was refused entry into the country and was forced to retrace his path back across the Atlantic. The travelling party was reduced by one. A monk of German nationality "felt the call of the Fatherland," as one newspaper put it, and decided to return to Germany instead.

Where a month before in Montreal Trebitsch had been the picture of affability, now he was bitter. He "pursed his lips in disgust" when reporters tried to interview him at Windsor Station. "Shuffle along" was all he would mutter to them as he got on the train.

His physical travels were pretty well now at an end, though perhaps not his spiritual ones. In 1933 the thirteenth Dalai Lama had died, followed four years later by his sometime rival the ninth Panchen Lama. A successor to the Dalai Lama, the current incumbent, had been recognized that same year but not yet enthroned, while no new Panchen Lama had yet been found. Into this vacuum stepped the Venerable Chao Kung. In 1938, Britain's embassy in China received a vague though delicious report that the one-time Montreal Presbyterian and Anglican, claiming to be the true reincarnation of both lamas, was on his way to Lhasa to claim his destiny.

Perhaps the journey, if it ever existed, was undertaken only in Chao Kung's imagination. Suffice it to say that he lived out the remainder of his astonishing life in Shanghai. It was there, with the city under Japanese occupation, that the man once known as Ignácz Trebitsch died on October 6, 1943.

One-time Montreal Presbyterian and Anglican Ignácz Trebitsch, aka Abbot Chao Kung, with his disciples. He claimed to be the reincarnation of two Tibetan lamas.
(*Montreal Daily Herald,* April 23, 1934.)

Chapter Five

~

So here it is at last, the distinguished thing.
. –Henry James, facing death, 1916

Spare a moment for Bernard Berté, Guillaume Boissier and Pierre Laforest. Their names ring no bells today, but they occupy a unique, albeit doleful, place in the history of Montreal. On June 9, 1643, they became the first of its citizens to die.

Not that men and women had never met their ends before where Montreal now stands. On and off for centuries, Indians had made their homes on the island. The village of Hochelaga that Jacques Cartier visited in 1535 was on the lower slopes of Mount Royal, though it seems to have disappeared by 1603 when François Gravé du Pont and Samuel de Champlain arrived. In the centuries since the coming of Europeans, the bones of aboriginal people, buried with evident reverence, have occasionally surfaced.

In the summer of 1898, for example, several ancient skeletons were discovered buried under the grounds of the St. George's Snowshoe Club in Westmount. One of them, of a slender woman perhaps twenty years old, was found beneath a pair of heavy stones, arched over her remains in an inverted V. The bones of animals had been ritually placed there as well, together with a single white bead. "As white wampum was the gift of a lover," historian W.D. Lighthall wrote at the time, perhaps a little fancifully, "this sole ornament tells the pathetic story of early love and death."

In 1611, Champlain returned to the future site of Montreal. He landed at Pointe à Callières, in today's Old Port, and stayed a week or so.

Clearly, he was planning how a permanent European settlement could be established. There was land that looked promising for crops, and good hunting nearby. It was the same site that Paul de Chomedey, Sieur de Maisonneuve, would choose for Ville Marie in 1642.

There was a young man in Champlain's party whom we know only as Louis. One day, this Louis went with two Indians on a hunting expedition to the top of the Lachine Rapids. They did well—so well, in fact, that the wildfowl they shot could scarcely all be loaded into their canoe. Yet one of the Indians, a Montagnais chief named Outetoucos, was reluctant to leave any of their bag behind. He insisted they shoot the rapids back to Champlain's camp, low gunwales and all.

It was a fatal mistake. No sooner were they into the boiling current than the overloaded canoe began to take on water. Louis panicked. Even though he could not swim, he leapt over the side and soon drowned. Moments later, Outetoucos tried to swim for shore and also drowned. Only Savignon, the other Indian, kept his head. The young Huron stayed with the wildly careering canoe, and so survived.

Louis was the first European to die within sight of Mount Royal. The old name attached to the rapids, Sault Saint-Louis, supposedly preserves his memory. Then, fourteen years later, a Récollet priest named Nicolas Viel was returning from the country of the Hurons to Quebec City. As his tiny flotilla was shooting the last of the rapids on the Rivière des Prairies, the three Indians paddling Viel's canoe murdered the priest —the reason is not clear—and threw his body overboard. A Huron boy named Ahuntsic who had been converted to Christianity by Viel was in a following canoe. He saw what had happened and he, too, was killed. Their names, like Louis's, echo today in the riverside communities of Ahuntsic and Sault-au-Récollet.

But what of the now-forgotten Bernard Berté, Guillaume Boissier and Pierre Laforest? In the late spring of 1643, de Maisonneuve's tiny settlement of Ville Marie—the future Montreal—was barely a year old. The three men, with three others, were working in an open space a hundred yards or so outside its frail perimeter. They were hard at it, cutting and sawing up wood, and didn't see about forty Mohawks rushing upon them until it was too late. In the brief struggle, Berté, Boissier and Laforest were cut down. The other three were captured and hustled back to the Mohawks' camp at Lachine.

The strong wind that day muffled any sound of the struggle. Only later, when the men had not returned as expected, did a patrol venture out from Ville Marie. They soon found Boissier's body in the clearing, those of the other two men a little way off in the bush. All three had been scalped.

Some Hurons, who had been anxious to ingratiate themselves with the Mohawks, were waiting at the Lachine camp when the raiding party returned. According to François Dollier de Casson, Montreal's earliest historian, "The Hurons ... passed the whole night insulting the Frenchmen"—that is, torturing them.

The following day, the Mohawks turned on their erstwhile Huron allies, killing most of them. Then they forced their terrified French captives into canoes and crossed to the other side of the St. Lawrence. They were bound for the Richelieu River, but along the way decided to pick up the pace by going overland. They cached some furs they had taken from the Hurons and abandoned several canoes, chopping holes in them to make them useless to anyone else. Farther on, however, they relaxed their watchfulness a little, thinking the three Frenchmen were now thoroughly cowed and disoriented, and this gave one of them a chance. He managed to slip away, found the damaged canoes, plugged the holes of one with fistfuls of grass and brought his horrifying story back to Ville Marie.

There, he found that Berté, Boissier and Laforest had already been buried in graves by the waterfront. It was the settlement's first cemetery, and its traces can still be seen in the crypt of the Centre d'Archéologie et d'Histoire de Montréal. The other two men, the French later learned, were tortured to death. The remains of their ravaged bodies were never found.

Such was the cloud—surprise attack, a sudden death for some, a lingering one for others—that would hang over Montreal for nearly sixty years, until the Great Peace of 1701. Even so, deadly peril might still await Montrealers who continued to venture beyond Iroquois territory, as Ezekiel Solomons and his partners, all Jewish, were to find out.

When the Seven Years' War broke out in 1756, he and Levy Solomons (apparently his cousin), Chapman Abraham, Benjamin Lyon and Gershon Levy went into business supplying the British army. After the fighting ended in 1760, Britain allowed Jews to enter what had been

New France, and the partners leapt at the chance. There were fortunes to be made, especially in trading for furs.

Montreal was their base. One day in 1761, Ezekiel Solomons—the same Solomons who, we have seen, would be throwing punches in Place d'Armes fourteen years later—landed at Fort Michilimackinac. The fort, where Lake Michigan meets Lake Huron, was still occupied by French and Canadians, stragglers from the war. About 200 Ottawas sympathetic to them were camped nearby. Solomons and several dozen other voyageurs who arrived with him were suddenly in deep trouble. Arguments broke out, then gunfire. The badly outnumbered traders took shelter and defended themselves as best they could. A massacre was averted only when British soldiers detailed to take over the fort arrived by a happy chance two days later.

If Solomons and his partners needed a reminder of how dangerous it could be up-country, this was it. Yet even when the Ottawa warchief Pontiac and his allies began attacking British garrisons two years later, they pressed on. Levy Solomons would soon pay for such bravado. In May of 1763, he and two other traders were captured near Fort Detroit by a band of Pontiac's warriors. A contemporary account says they were able to escape only after "remaining with the Indians for some time." There's nothing to indicate it was a restful sojourn.

Certainly it was not restful for Chapman Abraham when he, too, was captured near Fort Detroit that same month. He was tied by the waist and neck to a stake; his arms were left free, to flail about impotently. A fire was set in such a way as to burn as slowly as possible, and Abraham in his torment cried out for something to drink.

A missionary named John Heckewelder recorded what happened next:

> It is a custom of the Indians, previous to a prisoner being put to death, to give him what they call his last meal. A bowl of pottage or broth was therefore brought to him, for that purpose. Eager to quench his thirst, he put the bowl immediately to his lips, and the liquor being very hot, he was dreadfully scalded.
>
> Being a man of very quick temper, the moment he felt his mouth burned, he threw the bowl and its contents full in the

Chapman Abraham narrowly escapes being burned at the stake.
(Drawing by Harvey Dunn, *Saturday Evening Post*, May 14, 1938.)

Levy Solomons, c. 1780.
(Private Collection)

face of the man who handed it to him. "He is mad! He is mad!" resounded from all quarters. The bystanders considered his conduct as an act of insanity, and immediately untied the cords with which he was bound, and let him go where he pleased.

Pontiac's rebellion was nearly the end of Ezekiel Solomons as well. A few weeks after Abraham's close call, Solomons was back at Fort Michilimackinac, just in time for one of the most dramatic incidents in Canadian history. Outside the fort, Sauk and Chippewa warriors started a game of lacrosse and some of the Canadians and most of the British garrison went outside to watch. Foolishly, they left their weapons behind. Suddenly Madjeckewiss, the Chippewa chief, hurled the ball over the stockade and into the fort. Warriors from both tribes, knives and tomahawks in their hands, rushed the fort and the slaughter began.

Solomons was among a handful of traders who had remained behind in the fort. They tried to hide themselves but were soon discovered. Two days later, seven Chippewas took Solomons and three other white men off to the west. As one of them would later say, they were certain their captors wanted "only to kill and devour us." Luckily, they were saved when a band of Ottawas stopped the Chippewas' canoes and relieved them of their prisoners. It was not because the Ottawas were feeling especially charitable toward Solomons and his friends, only that they were offended the Chippewas had excluded them from the attack on the fort.

Gershon Levy arrived at the fort just after the massacre. He was captured and also abused and, like Solomons, was lucky to get back to Montreal. The five men had lost their trade goods, they were financially ruined and their partnership broke up. But they had their lives and they could rebuild. And so they did. By 1771, for example, Levy Solomons was one of Montreal's richest merchants. He and Ezekiel were among the founders of the town's first synagogue. So far as the available records show, they all died in their beds. It so easily could have been otherwise.

Men like Champlain in his *Voyages*, the authors of the *Jesuit Relations* and Dollier de Casson were merely the first of a long succession of European chroniclers to deplore Indian savagery. Yet the moral superiority such writers take on is ill-fitting. It's sobering to reflect that such enormities were not so very different from the European variety. Until well into the British regime, perfectly legal punishments for an astonishing number of crimes included flogging, branding, mutilation, burning at the stake and, as a follow-up to being hanged, disembowelment and dismemberment.

This harsh reality would catch up to Jean Baptiste Goyer *dit* Belisle in 1752. Goyer farmed on the Chemin du Roi, today's Boulevard René-Lévesque in Montreal. His farm was a little to the west of the track that has become Guy Street, where the Grey Nuns' mother house, now part of Concordia University, can be seen.

Not only was Goyer a rather lazy man, but he was jealous of the hardworking and prosperous Jean Favre, his neighbour. One night, he armed himself with a pistol and a knife and broke into Favre's house. Favre awoke, and the surprised Goyer fired his pistol, then finished him off with his knife. Favre's wife burst in and was herself stabbed, then beaten to death with a shovel. Goyer stepped past the bodies, helped himself to the money he knew Favre kept in a cupboard and slipped away into the darkness.

For weeks, the whole of Montreal, then a town of perhaps 4,000 people, talked of little else but the sensational crime. In such a climate, Goyer was stupid in the extreme to flaunt his sudden wealth. He was arrested and subjected first to the *question ordinaire,* that is, normal interrogation. When this failed to yield a confession, it was time for the *question extraordinaire,* a euphemism for torture.

This usually consisted of strapping boards to the victim's legs, then inserting wedges and pounding the boards with a hammer. Each blow was likely to crush some bone; after each blow, a question would be put to the agonized victim.

However it was done to Goyer, he confessed in due course and was condemned to be broken on the wheel. On the day of his execution, he was taken to the marketplace at what's now Place Royale. He was made to mount a scaffold and then was tied to a wagon wheel. His kidneys, his arms and what was left of his shins and thighs were shattered with heavy blows. "His face turned to the sky," he was left to die slowly.

Afterward, his broken body was ignominiously buried at the crossroads by the scene of his crime. A cross painted blood-red was erected as a reminder of the appalling fate that murderers could expect.

The cross stood well into the nineteenth century until it was replaced around 1870 by the crucifix that remains in front of the mother house to this day.

Exemplary death of a much different sort came calling on Montreal during the typhus epidemic of 1847. Other epidemics have staggered the city, notably cholera in 1832, smallpox in 1885 and influenza in 1918, but the typhus of 1847 is probably the most iconic for Montrealers.

Overwhelmingly, its victims were thousands of Irish immigrants, Catholic and wretchedly poor. But inevitably, it also took a toll among the doctors, religious, soldiers, civic officials and others—surely no more than a couple of hundred—who selflessly sought to help them.

The Irish were fleeing the potato famine that ravaged their homeland in the mid-1840s. They hoped for survival in the New World, little suspecting that another mortal danger awaited them on the decrepit "coffin ships" in which they sailed. When they crowded on board, many already bore the highly infectious typhus organism, and at least 8,000 of them died long before they saw land again. Thousands more succumbed in quarantine on Grosse Île, and on the waterfront at Quebec City and Montreal.

By June, it was clear that Montreal was on the brink of disaster. The flood of people—and of infection—was relentless. On some of the ships that arrived, the dead seemed to outnumber the living. A few souls in the last stages of the disease were brusquely dumped ashore and left to die, their feet quite literally never having touched the promised land they sought.

Mayor John Easton Mills ordered the construction of sheds at Point St. Charles as hospitals and temporary housing for the immigrants. These were the so-called fever sheds, each about fifty yards long. At first it seemed that three would be enough; eventually, twenty-two were built. They were soon foul and stinking. The sick lay next to the dying and, all too often, the dead, rotting in their own sweat, vomit, pus and feces. Shamefully, some Montrealers came to the Point to gawk at the spectacle, from a discreet distance, of course, while others ranted that the sheds and the people they sheltered should be pushed into the river. A mob of protesters meeting on the Champ de Mars threatened to do just that. They rushed to the waterfront, but Mayor Mills and a detachment of police got there first. Arms linked, they managed to face down their anger.

Mayor Mills was not alone. There were others whom we must honour, among them Father Jackson John Richards. Born in the United States and ordained in Montreal in 1813, he made the care of the city's few English-speaking Catholics his particular concern. When their numbers suddenly began to swell in 1847, he did not hesitate. He and his fellow priests from the newly opened St. Patrick's Church were down at the sheds every day, doing what they could to relieve the suffering.

Father Patrick Morgan was the first of them to die, on July 8. Three more from St. Patrick's followed in the next week. And finally, on July 23, a Friday, it was Father Richards's turn.

The Gazette said the toll that Friday alone had been 1,626 people lying ill in the sheds, and another thirty-three dead. Immediately beneath that report was a letter to the editor from a man signing himself simply as "B." It seems that some time before, B had been sitting with a merchant named Yarwood who, at one point, got up to leave his office. Just then, someone else came in to say that Father Richards needed some bedding straw for the fever victims he was tending.

"A load of straw for Father Richards?" Yarwood exclaimed. "I wish I could give him a load of gold!"

Yarwood then left his office, for the last time as it turned out. Shortly afterward he fell ill and soon died—though from the notoriously rapid onslaught of typhus or from some other cause was not stated.

Now, with Father Richards dead as well, B was prompted to write. "There was a fervency in (Yarwood's) expression which imposed the words on my memory," he concluded his letter, "and now, what a comment on human wishes. They are both gone to where the gold and the straw of this world are alike valueless."

In recording Father Richards's fate, The Gazette also noted that "the whole of the sisters of the Grey Nunnery, we regret to say, are laid up with illness contracted in the same mission." Several weeks before, their superior, Mother Elizabeth McMullen, had gone down to the sheds to assess the situation for herself. She was horrified. Returning to the convent, she assembled the nuns before her, some forty in all.

"Sisters, I have seen a sight today that I shall never forget," she told them. "I went to Point St. Charles and found hundreds of sick and dying huddled together. The stench emanating from them is too great for even the strongest constitution. The atmosphere is impregnated with it, and the air filled with the groans of the sufferers. Death is there in its most appalling aspect. Those who thus cry aloud in their agony are strangers, but their hands are outstretched for relief."

Then came more ominous words: "Sisters, the plague is contagious. In sending you there I am signing your death warrant, but you are free to accept or refuse."

With scarcely a moment's hesitation, they all rose and each said, "I am ready." Mother McMullen chose eight, and the next day they were at work in the sheds. As more immigrants arrived in succeeding days, more of the Grey Nuns joined them. Death began to claim them late in July, and their places were taken by the Sisters of Providence. Bishop Ignace Bourget gave the cloistered nursing sisters of the Hôtel-Dieu special dispensation to join the struggle, and they did. Then, in September, with seven of their sisters in their graves, those Grey Nuns who by then had recovered returned to the sheds.

Protestant clergymen volunteered, and Rev. Mark Willoughby of Trinity Anglican Church was among those who died. His fellow Anglican, Jacob Ellegood, later the rector of St. James the Apostle, survived and would long remember serving in the fever sheds: "I saw them dying by the dozen, by the score. While I bent over them to take a last message, they died. While I held their hands, they died."

But Catholics felt a special obligation to serve, and Bishop Bourget led by example, spending alternate nights in the sheds with his vicar general. Indeed, the prelate was himself stricken, though he did recover. Like the young Jacob Ellegood, the Catholic priests placed themselves in particular danger, obligated as they were to bring their faces within inches of the fevered breath of the dying to hear their confessions. So many shared the fate of Father Richards and the other English-speaking priests that a special appeal was made to New York. Two Jesuits from Fordham University, Father Michael Driscoll and Father du Merle, were soon on their way.

As the summer gave way to cooler weather, the plague began to abate. Yet though they had already run appalling risks, many of the volunteers felt bound to continue their work. Among these was Mayor

Mills, who day after day could still be seen in the sheds, helping the sick to a few sips of water, rearranging their scraps of bedding, doing what he could to console the dying. His dedication caught up with him in November. It seemed an especially cruel fate, with the typhus he had done so much to fight by then virtually gone. He died on November 12.

Signposts commemorate many of Montreal's mayors. There is Rue Viger downtown, named after Jacques Viger, the city's first mayor. Honoré Beaugrand's name is on a street as well as a Métro station. Driving down the east side of Mount Royal, you will follow Voie Camillien-Houde, and perhaps stop to enjoy the view from the belvedere that also bears his name. The former Parc des Îles, on Île Sainte-Hélène and Île Notre-Dame, has been renamed to honour Jean Drapeau, whose greatest triumph, Expo 67, took place there.

But for the saintly John Easton Mills, there is nothing but a dinky little one-block street just east of the railway yards in the borough of Mercier/Hochelaga-Maisonneuve. Oh, it's on the waterfront, all right, but several miles away from where he so courageously offered his life in the service of others. Adding to the shame, the city didn't get around to devising even so meagre a memorial as this until just a handful of years ago.

Nonetheless, the sacrifice of Mayor Mills and all the other volunteers of 1847 remains undimmed by the passage of years. So does Sarah Maxwell's.

She was a young woman of thirty-one, the principal of Hochelaga School on Rue Préfontaine—just a few blocks from today's Rue John-Easton-Mills, as it happens. Early in the afternoon of February 26, 1907, she was teaching a math lesson when a boy named Willie Gilbert burst into her ground-floor classroom. "Fire!" he exclaimed. Fire had broken out in the basement.

She paused but a moment. It was a bitterly cold day, but no time could be wasted to put on hats and coats. With the smell of smoke suddenly all too evident, she quickly began to push her class out the door and ordered the children to run home. Then she ran back inside.

The scene there was rapidly becoming chaotic. There were four classrooms in the rather ramshackle building, two on each floor, and about 150 students all told. The older ones on the ground floor had an easier time getting out, but upstairs it was appallingly different.

A wood furnace in the basement heated the school, and the fire was likely started by several boys who had been playing with matches near the stacked firewood. It spread with terrible speed, fanned by a draft rushing up the rubbish chute from the basement to the upper floors.

Thick, choking smoke was rising fast to the second storey. There were no fire escapes. Some of the children stood frozen in terror at the top of the narrow stairway leading to safety. Finally, showing courage beyond his years, a boy named Tom Hogan pushed through them and started down the stairs, urging the others to follow. The spell was broken, and they would live. Other children stayed put, huddled beneath their desks, and many of them would die.

Three men working in an icehouse across the street, Moïse Rainville, Théophile Carignan and William Walsh, saw the commotion. Carignan ran to turn in the alarm, then joined the other two who had propped a ladder against the wall up to the second storey. Other men with ladders followed them. Inside the school, their hands bloody from breaking through the window glass, their lungs filling with the deadly smoke, Sarah Maxwell and the other three teachers began handing the children out, one by one.

Fire bells could be heard but—alas—the firemen themselves could not yet be seen. First, a horse new to the task balked shortly after the rig it was pulling left the station, and it took some time to get it going again. Then a streetcar got in the way. One of the reels was delayed when it struck a curb. And when they finally arrived, the firemen discovered the nearby hydrants were frozen.

By then, though the fire had truly taken hold, most of the children were out. A young fire captain named Christopher Carson, later to become chief for all of Montreal, set up several more ladders, and his men managed to pull out one of the teachers. They were in the nick of time: her dress was just beginning to catch fire. Then another teacher was rescued, and a third who had fainted.

At the top of a ladder, another captain named Ernest Benoît, with Carson just behind him, saw that Sarah Maxwell was still inside. She handed them a child, who was hurriedly passed down, then another and another. It could not go on. "Oh! I am burning!" she cried.

Benoît grabbed for the young woman's arm. "I got her!" he shouted to Carson. Squeezing up beside Benoît, he pleaded with her to save herself but she refused. There were more children still trapped inside, she shouted. She pulled away, her dress ripping in Carson's hand, and plunged back into the smoke.

As she disappeared there was an explosion, which drove Benoît and Carson back down the ladder. When it was pulled away from the wall, its top was on fire.

Benoît, Carson and their men steadily brought the blaze under control. Only then could they dare to go inside. The thousands of people who had gathered in the street groaned each time a bundle was brought out; no one needed to be told what it was. In all, the fire claimed sixteen children, the oldest just eight years old. The youngest was three. She was Mabel Spraggs and not even a pupil. She had been sent to the school that day with her five-year-old sister, Myrtle, to keep her out of the way of preparations for a wedding at home. The two little girls died in each other's arms.

Among the last bodies to be brought out of the ruined building was Sarah Maxwell's. She was the fire's seventeenth victim.

Her funeral was held two days later. When the cortege left the Rue Saint-Urbain house where she lived with her mother, it was preceded by twelve mounted police and a detachment of firemen. A vast throng of people fell in behind the flower-decked hearse, while others lined the long route to Christ Church Cathedral.

The cathedral was packed, and many had to stand in the aisles. "Conspicuous on every hand were the school children," a newspaper reported. "In all parts of the edifice, they were gathered in little groups." Later she was buried in Mount Royal Cemetery in a plot donated by cemetery trustees. Her heroism was commemorated in a plaque set up in the cathedral. And the following year, the burned-out shell of Hochelaga School was torn down, to be replaced by a new building. It was named Sarah Maxwell Memorial School.

Pathos is not limited to tragedies on the scale of the fire in Hochelaga, of course. Consider what befell the Ladouceur sisters in 1895.

Montreal in May of that year was unusually warm. There was extra vitality in the scent of the now snow-free earth and of the flowers coming into bloom. Yet where Léandre-Joseph Descaries lived, there was something else in the air.

Descaries was a prosperous notary with a comfortable house in Notre-Dame-de-Grâce. Early that month, he began to puzzle over a strange odour there. More than strange, it was fetid, yet with an odd sweetness, and what once were occasional whiffs had become a steady presence. Try as he might, he could no longer fool himself that it was from something rotting outside. The source had to be in the house, and he determined to find out exactly where.

The smell was strongest in the bathroom—and, as Descaries found when dropping to his knees, strongest of all at floor level. He was all set to take up the floorboards in his search, but first there was a small trap door to be checked out. It was less than four inches wide but "large enough," *The Gazette* reported, "to produce a clue to the mystery that had been the talk of the household for the past few days."

Descaries put his hand into the hole and felt something. It was soft and yielding, unlike anything he had touched before. He began to pull it out and discovered, to his horror, that he was holding the decomposing body of a tiny baby.

But whose? Suspicion instantly fell on two young women, Agnès Ladouceur and her younger sister, Ozala. Early that year, Descaries had hired them as domestic servants. He failed to notice, either then or later, that Ozala was pregnant.

Later, at the inquest into the baby's death, another servant testified that on April 3 Ozala complained she was unwell and could not work. Agnès went out and bought some medicine before spending the night with her. Clearly, Ozala was in labour. She gave birth to a little boy sometime before dawn.

The autopsy was conducted on May 7 by Dr. Wyatt Johnston of the Montreal General Hospital. He was only thirty-six but already had a formidable reputation as a forensic pathologist. He said the infant had been carried nearly to term and appeared normal in all respects. Though there was some flattening of the skull on one side, this probably resulted from his being thrust into the cramped hiding place beneath the bathroom floor.

The baby had not been stillborn, though how long he had lived or precisely how he had died Johnston could not say. But he did find that "on removing the scalp, a line of fracture is seen to extend one inch into the upper border of the right parietal bone. The parts adjoining this fracture are somewhat reddened. ... Just posterior to the fracture is a small defect in the bone half-inch deep, with sharp smooth edges."

Otherwise, there was no indication of violence. Nor was there any sign of bruising. But because the body's soft tissues had deteriorated so much, Johnston could not rule out the possibility that there had once been some. That was enough to charge the sisters with murder.

However sensational this build-up, the trial five months later was an anticlimax. So compelling were the lawyers for the defence, E.N. Saint-Jean and Charles Archer, that the jury felt no need to leave the box. The day after the trial opened it closed, with Agnès and Ozala not guilty.

Perhaps the child died from neglect—but that was not the crime with which the Ladouceurs were charged. Perhaps the jury came to believe that, shortly after birth, the infant died of natural causes the pathologist had not detected. Or consider the cracked skull: perhaps, in panic, Ozala had accidentally, and fatally, dropped her newborn son.

This much we can conclude, however. It seems plain that Ozala was pregnant out of wedlock, and her prospects as a young, unwed mother in late Victorian Montreal would not have been glowing. There were signs, nonetheless, that she and Agnès were going to try. The examination of the baby's large intestine showed he had been nursed: the women were not about to let him starve.

Four years later, in 1899, the streets of Montreal would see their first automobile, making inevitable a new way of dying. It took another seven years to happen, but on August 11, 1906, Antoine Toutant became the city's first auto fatality.

Toutant, a forty-seven-year-old labourer, was with his wife, Emma, and their fourteen-year-old son on Ste. Catherine Street East. They were near the corner of Alexandre-de-Sève. Deciding to cross to the north side, they stepped in front of a stopped streetcar. Suddenly, Emma became aware of something rapidly bearing down on them from the left. As she darted across Ste. Catherine, Antoine made to follow her, was briefly held back by their son, then broke free. It was a fatal move. A car knocked him down, and his skull was fractured as he hit the pavement. One of the wheels passed over his body.

The car was driven by a man named Thomas Atkinson. He

immediately stopped and helped carry Toutant to a nearby drugstore. An ambulance took him to Notre Dame Hospital where he died twenty minutes after his arrival.

Today, such a story might merit a paragraph or two in the newspapers, no more. But in 1906, there were perhaps 250 cars in the whole of Quebec. So unusual was Toutant's death that two stories of considerable length were to appear in *The Gazette*, one on the accident itself and another on the subsequent inquest.

The novelty of automobiles was plain at the inquest. Witnesses were hard-pressed to testify about the speed of Atkinson's except in terms of horses. A boy named Alfred Saint-Charles would say only that it was going faster than a trotting horse. Joseph Boivin, a carter, was more certain. Based on his experience with horses, he said, the car was doing about twenty miles per hour. Another witness, Jean-Baptiste-Octave Lescarbeau, guessed thirty or thirty-five miles per hour, "but anyway it was going faster than a horse."

Atkinson was found criminally negligent, held without bail and remanded to August 21. Unfortunately, news of his fate has not been preserved. However, lest there be any doubt that a new age was dawning, there was another fatal accident, almost certainly the second in Montreal, just six days after the one that killed Toutant.

The circumstances were similar. A car driven by one Herbert Pocock was heading west on Boulevard Saint-Joseph in Lachine. As it approached the locks at the upstream end of the Lachine Canal, Pocock saw a wagon in the centre of the road, moving slowly in the same direction. He tooted his horn, but the teamster took no notice. Pocock decided to pass, but as he pulled abreast of the horses, a boy dashed across the roadway in front of them. His name was Sarsfield Fleming, and he was just seven years old.

The car's mudguard knocked the boy to the ground, and Pocock immediately stopped. A passenger, James Allan, picked up the crumpled body and carried it to a nearby house. A doctor was called but to no avail. The boy could not be saved.

At the inquest, Allan said the car was going no faster than perhaps six miles per hour and that Pocock was able to stop the car before it had even passed the boy's prostrate form. That hardly seems fast enough to have killed someone, even with the small frame of a seven-year-old. Plainly, dreadful misfortune was at work, and even Sarsfield's father said he was satisfied there had been no negligence. The verdict was not long in coming: "excusable homicide."

Dreadful misfortune was also the fate of Robert Patrick. He was forty-eight years old, by all reports an utterly blameless resident of Verdun with a job in a stockbroker's office downtown.

One May evening in 1934, Patrick was sitting peacefully in the second-floor flat on Rue de l'Église that he shared with his wife. Her parents lived in the flat immediately above, and that evening her mother happened to be visiting. She was a couple of rooms away when she suddenly heard a tremendous crash. It sounded like an earthquake, she thought, but on rushing to the front room she saw how wrong she had been. Robert Patrick had been struck by some bizarre object and was obviously dead.

"His head was almost cut in two," a newspaper would report, seeming to savour every Grand Guignol detail, "and the missile, its strength almost spent, crashed into the wall and bounced back onto the victim, bespattering him with his blood."

Screaming in horror, the woman ran to the rear gallery. Neighbours called a doctor, who in turn called the police.

When Patrick's body was eventually taken away to the morgue, his feet were still crossed. Quite literally, he never knew what hit him, and for a while no one else did either.

Detective Sergeants A. Sevigny and Wilfrid Liot of the Verdun force were soon on the scene. Their eyes were drawn to the strange piece of metal on the sofa beside Patrick. Above, they could see a gaping hole in the ceiling and another in the ceiling of his in-laws' flat beyond. On the floor was another clue, a white powder that for a moment led them to think a bomb had been hurled into the building. It turned out to be plaster dust.

The piece of metal that struck Patrick was disk-like and weighed about twenty-four pounds. It seemed weird, but could it have been a wheel that fell from an airplane flying overhead? Quick calls to the airfields at Cartierville and Saint-Hubert squelched that idea. No planes were reported to have been in the vicinity.

Then another idea, no less weird, began to push its way forward. Sevigny and Liot knew there were some small lumberyards nearby. Perhaps the lethal piece of metal had somehow been thrown from one of the saws.

They began to snoop about the neighbourhood. First one sawmill, then another, showed no sign of damaged machinery. But then, scrambling over a fence surrounding a third mill, they found what they were looking for. It was the backyard of one Isadore Lavoie who, together with his son René and an employee named Irénée Tremblay, had a circular saw hard at work. It was a crude, homemade contraption, powered by a belt running from the rear axle of a propped-up pickup truck.

Lavoie was nothing if not insouciant. Something, he supposed, had happened a little while before when a piece of metal had flown off the saw toward the Aqueduct and Côte Saint-Paul. But—hey—the saw was still working, so what was all the fuss about?

Fuss, indeed. The two detectives soon found that chunks had been flung from Lavoie's machine in at least four directions. In addition to the piece he admitted to, a second had gone through a fence and imbedded itself in a hydro pole. A third left holes in the roof and wall of a nearby shed before splashing down in the nearby waterworks reservoir. The fourth, and heaviest of all, was the piece that killed Robert Patrick.

The inquest was held three days later, and by law its jury had to view the body. By then it had been returned to the Patrick flat and laid out for the wake. To add to the distress of the man's family and friends, the jury showed up in the midst of the gathering, which could resume only after they had done their macabre duty.

Later, after deliberating just a few minutes, the jury returned a verdict of accidental death. Pierre Hébert, the deputy coroner, recommended that in future small sawmills like Lavoie's be required to obtain provincial licences, but that was all. It surely was small comfort to Patrick's widow.

Like Robert Patrick, Charlie Feigenbaum was also forty-eight years old and, within a few months, was just as dead. But far from being a picture of blameless rectitude, Feigenbaum was a lifelong hoodlum. Honour among thieves meant little to him. He made the mistake of crossing the legendary crime boss Harry Davis, and he paid with his life.

In August 1934, the overweight, cigar-chomping Feigenbaum was living on Boulevard Saint-Joseph in Montreal. Early one evening he drove over to the apartment of his brother Maxie at the corner of Boulevard Mont-Royal and Avenue de l'Esplanade. He was to pick up some boxes of clothing, though in his stylish grey suit jacket and plus-fours he hardly looked dressed for donkey work. Within minutes, it didn't matter.

He was handing the boxes through the window of his car to his eighteen-year-old son, Jackie. Neither of them took much notice of the powerful Hudson sedan idling at the curb across the street. It was brand new and painted an ominous black.

There were three men inside. One of them got out and crossed the street. Without saying a word, he steadied his aim on the hood of Feigenbaum's car, emptied a revolver into his startled victim, then dashed back to the Hudson. The car roared off along Esplanade, the hitman perched precariously on the running board. Feigenbaum, with at least one bullet in his heart, lay dead on the pavement. Fee for the hit: $250.

Four years before, Feigenbaum had been a trusted member of Harry Davis's mob. Davis, born Chaskel Lazarovitch in Romania in 1898, had come to Canada as a boy and soon found ways to make crime pay. By his mid-twenties, he and another crook, Pincus Brecher, had a steely grip on some of Montreal's best nightclubs and gambling dens. Feigenbaum was in charge of hundreds of slot machines in hotels in the Laurentians.

But though he was called the King of the North, Feigenbaum knew he was just a mere lieutenant. He wanted to run his own show. Buying off some customs officials, he began smuggling high-ticket items into the country without paying duty. But then he got caught. In 1930, a $100,000 shipment of silk netted him not a tidy profit but five years in prison.

According to Feigenbaum, Davis swore he would look after his family. But while behind bars, he learned that Davis was not only ignoring that promise but cutting him loose as well. This double betrayal was too much. To get even, he made a deal, trading what he knew about Davis's operation, including Brecher's part in it, for an early release.

And so it was that in April 1933, Davis was arrested for trafficking a staggering 852 kilos of heroin and other drugs in 1930 alone. Thanks in large part to his one-time subordinate's testimony, Davis was found guilty and sentenced to fourteen years and ten strokes of the lash. Feigenbaum, his coat well turned, was back on the street early in 1934. With Davis instead of him now behind bars, he figured he could comfortably ease his way back into his old haunts and his old ways. But he was ready to play the other side of the street as well, agreeing to help the Crown by testifying at Brecher's drug trial the following September.

Feigenbaum wasn't entirely a fool. Just to be sure, he kept a bodyguard near his side and a pistol in his pocket. Nonetheless, he woefully under-estimated how deep was Davis's wrath and how much of the Montreal underworld he still controlled from behind the bars of his cell.

Early in August, a pair of hired killers traced the once and would-be future King of the North to Val-Morin. But they had also been given a sketchy description of Maxie Feigenbaum and weren't sure which of the brothers they had in their sights. They didn't pull the trigger. Charlie Feigenbaum never learned of that close call, nor that the inevitable had been put off by a mere two weeks. The last day of his life was the first he had gone out without his bodyguard.

It was one of the first gangland rub-outs in a city that has since seen many. Some hours afterward, the Hudson was found abandoned nearby and was eventually traced to a dealership on Rue Saint-Denis. It had been sold three weeks before to someone named L. Bercowitz on Guy Street, but the address turned out to be a phoney. Bercowitz was never found, and the trail to Feigenbaum's killers eventually faded away.

Whatever satisfaction Davis enjoyed from Feigenbaum's demise, it didn't do Brecher much good. Feigenbaum wasn't available to testify, of course, but what he had to say about Brecher during the Davis trial was on the record. Brecher was found guilty and knew he faced a lengthy stay in prison.

He didn't wait to find out just how long. Remanded to Bordeaux Jail to await sentencing, Brecher was being led by guards along a catwalk serving the third-tier level of cells. Suddenly he broke loose and threw himself over the railing. He died on the steel plates of the floor beneath.

In 1945, Davis was granted an early release. Other crime bosses had come onto the scene, but Davis still had a lot of clout. Soon he was once again Montreal's gambling kingpin.

The following year, a man came to Davis's headquarters on Stanley Street and asked for permission to set up a bookmaking business. Davis turned him down, saying the field was already too crowded. If the man went ahead anyway, Davis warned, he "could be taken care of just as easily as Feigenbaum." On July 25, the man returned, pulled out a pistol and shot Davis dead. The man's name was Louis Bercovitch, tantalizingly similar to the "L. Bercowitz" who had bought that Hudson twelve years before. He claimed he killed Davis not because his ambitions had been stymied but because he had heard the crime boss had hired a gunman from New York to kill him. His only way out, Bercovitch said, was to kill Davis first.

Bercovitch pleaded guilty to manslaughter and was sentenced to life in prison, but was released after serving eleven-and-a-half years. Despite the apparent links to Charlie Feigenbaum's murder in 1934, it was the only shooting for which he was ever charged.

Envoi

~

In Montreal there is no present tense, there is only
the past claiming victories.
–Leonard Cohen, "The Favourite Game," 1963

Many pages ago, at the beginning of this book, I suggested that in a sense Montreal was the true capital of Canada, thanks to the weight of the city's history. In fact, for six years it really was the seat of national government.

Starting in 1844 Parliament sat in St. Ann's Market, a long and rather handsome two-storey building in the middle of Youville Square. The country, properly called the Province of Canada, consisted of what's now southern Quebec and Ontario. It was still a British colony, though with considerable powers to run its own internal affairs. Early in 1849, this Parliament passed the Rebellion Losses Bill to compensate property owners in Lower Canada for losses suffered during the Patriote rebellions of 1837 and 1838. The bill, however, made no distinction between those who supported the Patriotes and those who had remained loyal. Many, especially among English-speaking Montrealers, were furious.

On April 25, 1849, the governor general, Lord Elgin, arrived at Parliament to give royal assent to the bill. Whatever reservations he might have had, he was determined to encourage responsible government, a new departure for the colony, by heeding the will of the elected representatives. He signed the bill. But afterward, when he came out of the building, he found a mob had gathered. Insults were shouted. Eggs were thrown, one of which struck Elgin in the face, and his mounted military

Burning of the Parliament, Youville Square, night of April 25, 1849.
(Illustration by Martin Somerville, *Illustrated London News*, May 19, 1849)

escort was fortunate to get him back to his home at Monklands in one piece.

That night, the mob descended on Youville Square, burst into Parliament and ransacked it. A fire broke out, and by dawn the building was a smoking ruin. Appalled, the legislators invited Elgin to return to the city a few days later, to his office at the Château Ramezay, where they would offer a formal apology. No coward, Elgin did so, only to find, once again in the street after the brief ceremony, that the mob had returned. This time rocks were among the missiles, and several landed in the carriage. Again, he was lucky to get away unharmed.

For years at the Elgin family seat in Scotland, there was a small box containing two rough stones. A label, in Lady Elgin's hand, reads, "Thrown at the Govr Genl—Montreal, April 30—1849." His great-grandson, the eleventh earl, once told me the stones occupy "pride of place" among the family's Canadian souvenirs: "They undoubtedly led to a fuller understanding of parliamentary democracy, and must have a very special place in the history of the British Empire." The family recently donated the stones to the people of Canada.

Meanwhile, back in Montreal, disturbances of one sort or another continued for months. A disgusted Elgin had come to feel that the city was rotten to the core, and late that year the capital was moved to Toronto. Then, on the last day of 1857, it moved a final time, to the newly renamed lumber town of Ottawa.

But what if it had been otherwise? What if the mob had merely shouted its slogans and then gone home, leaving both Parliament and Elgin's dignity intact and the capital unchanged? What stories might now be drawn from Montreal's history. Imagine this:

July 1, 1867: A brilliant day of festivities marking the birth of Confederation concluded with an evening show of fireworks arching into the sky over Canada's newly constructed Parliament Buildings. The dramatic site of the buildings on Île Sainte-Hélène was shown to advantage. Thousands of citizens swarmed over the Pont Concordia, linking Place Jacques-Cartier with the island, in order to cheer their approval.

July 1, 1892: The prime minister, Sir John J.C. Abbott, presided over the inauguration of the Dominion Tower high atop Mount Royal, twenty-five years to the day after the birth of the Confederation it commemorates. He said he was proud that so graceful a structure would now ornament the city he had called home for most of his life.

The much-delayed project was a favourite of Abbott's predecessor, the late Sir John A. Macdonald. An allegorical figure symbolizing Canada stands on a tall, slender column, and the bowl-like structure she holds has quickly though irreverently come to be known as Macdonald's Tassie. Seven additional figures reclining at the base of the column represent the provinces, with space left for at least six more.

May 10, 1932: In his speech from the throne, Governor General Henri Bourassa paid tribute to the distinctive new Canadian flag, which replaced the Union Jack and flew from the Peace Tower above him for the first time. A colourful honour guard was drawn up in front of the Parliament Buildings, and the 21-gun salute of a field battery on Mount Royal could be heard throughout the city. Although protocol naturally prevented Bourassa from making any personal remarks about the flag, the first native-born governor general of confederated Canada must have been pleased. After all, in the Quebec legislature, in Parliament and as editor of Le Devoir, he has long fought for a vigorously independent Canada offering an equal place to French and English.

Bourassa also said the government has decided to construct a new building for the Supreme Court of Canada on one of the most desirable building sites in Montreal. The courthouse will be erected over the "hole" on Dorchester Street where the CNR tracks emerge from the Mount Royal Tunnel. The vast and embarrassing crater has long defaced the centre of the national capital.

February 1, 1955: The Bank of Toronto and the Dominion Bank of Canada, whose merger has just taken effect, announced that the new institution's head office would be moved from Toronto to Montreal. Bank officials were blunt. They said that the post-war concentration of commercial and banking power in Montreal was continuing and that they could not offer their most important clients the service they deserved while based in a mere provincial capital.

June 23, 1990: Canadian premiers started returning to their homes from the federal government retreat at Lac Brôme outside Montreal, conscious of having made history. The Brome Lake Accord, which they all signed, recognizes French and English Canada alike as distinct societies. It is a typically Canadian compromise that shows signs of crippling what was threatening to become a well-established national industry, constitutional reform.

May 2, 2002: The federal government announced that to help the economically depressed eastern part of Ontario, it would shift yet another section of the Public Works Department—47 clerks and middle managers in all—from Montreal to Bytown.

Suggestions for Further Reading

This book, making no pretence of being a formal academic history, contains no footnotes, exhaustive bibliography or other scholarly apparatus. Undeniably, however, I have consulted many works written for both scholarly and popular readerships, as well as diaries, old newspapers, original historical records and other material. Where it seemed appropriate, I have indicated a source in the body of my narrative.

Here, and with a bias toward the popular rather than the scholarly, are some suggestions for further reading:

Collard, Edgar Andrew, *Canadian Yesterdays* (1955).

——. *Montreal Yesterdays* (1962).

——. *Call Back Yesterdays* (1965).

——. *Montreal: the Days That Are No More* (1976).

——. *All Our Yesterdays* (1988).

——. *Montreal Yesterdays: More Stories from All Our Yesterdays* (1989).

——. *100 More Tales from All Our Yesterdays* (1990).

Dollier de Casson, François, *A History of Montreal 1640-1672*, trans. Ralph Flenley (1928).

Jenkins, Kathleen, *Montreal: Island City of the St. Lawrence* (1966).

Prévost, Robert, *Montréal: a History*, trans. Elizabeth Mueller and Robert Chodos (1993).

Robert, Jean-Claude, *Atlas Historique de Montréal* (1994).

Roberts, Leslie, *Montreal: From Mission Colony to World City* (1969).

Rumilly, Robert, *Histoire de Montréal*, 5 vols. (1970).

Weintraub, William, *City Unique: Montreal Days and Nights in the 1940s and '50s.* (1996).

In addition, I found it especially useful to consult the following:

Adams, Frank Dawson, *A History of Christ Church Cathedral Montreal* (1941).

Alberts, Robert C., *The Most Extraordinary Adventures of Major Robert Stobo* (1965).

Betcherman, Lita-Rose, *The Swastika and the Maple Leaf: Fascist Movements in Canada in the Thirties* (1975).

Bliss, Michael, *Plague: A Story of Smallpox in Montreal* (1991).

Burt, Alfred Leroy, *The Old Province of Quebec*, 2 vols. (1968).

Cole, J.A., *Prince of Spies: Henri Le Caron* (1984).

Cooper, John Irwin, *The Blessed Communion: The Origins and History of the Diocese of Montreal 1760-1960* (1960).

de Lagrave, Jean-Paul, *Voltaire's Man in America*, trans. Arnold Bennett (1997).

Demos, John, *The Unredeemed Captive: A Family Story from Early America* (1994).

Donaldson, Frances, *Edward VIII* (1974).

English, John and Réal Bélanger, current eds., *Dictionary of Canadian Biography*, 15 vols. (1966-2006).

Fleming, R.B., *The Railway King of Canada: Sir William Mackenzie 1849-1923* (1991).

Godfrey, Rupert, ed., *Letters from a Prince: Edward Prince of Wales to Mrs. Freda Dudley Ward March 1918 – January 1921* (1998).

Godfrey, Sheldon J. and Judith C. Godfrey, *Search Out the Land: The Jews and the Growth of Equality in British Colonial America 1740-1867* (1995).

Harvison, C.W., *The Horsemen* (1967).

Hoy, Claire, *Canadians in the Civil War* (2004).

Lambert, Phyllis and Alan Stewart, eds., *Opening the Gates of Eighteenth-Century Montréal* (1992).

Lanctot, Gustave, *Montreal Under Maisonneuve 1642-1665*, trans. Alta Lind Cook (1969).

MacDonnell, Tom, *Daylight Upon Magic: The Royal Tour of Canada – 1939* (1989).

MacKay, Donald, *Anticosti: The Untamed Island* (1979).

Marsan, Jean-Claude, *Montreal in Evolution,* trans. Arnaud de Varent (1981).

Mayers, Adam, *Dixie and the Dominion: Canada, the Confederacy and the War for the Union* (2003).

Medres, Israel, *Montreal of Yesterday: Jewish Life in Montreal 1900-1920,* trans. Vivian Felsen (2000).

Neatby, Hilda, *Quebec: the Revolutionary Age 1760-1791* (1966).

Ouellet, Fernand, *Lower Canada 1791-1840: Social Change and Nationalism* (1980).

Porter, McKenzie, *Julie: the Royal Mistress* (1961).

Preston, Richard Arthur, ed., *For Friends at Home: A Scottish Emigrant's Letters from Canada, California and the Cariboo 1844-1864* (1974).

Radforth, Ian, *Royal Spectacle: the 1860 Visit of the Prince of Wales to Canada and the United States* (2004).

Robertson, J. Ross, ed., *The Diary of Mrs. John Graves Simcoe* (2001).

Sellar, Robert, *The History of the County of Huntingdon and of the Seigniories of Chateauguay and Beauharnois* (1888).

Shepherd, Francis J., *Origin and History of the Montreal General Hospital* (n.d.).

Simpson, Patricia, *Marguerite Bourgeoys and Montreal 1640-1665* (1997).

Stanley, George F.G., *Canada Invaded 1775-1776* (1977).

Toker, Franklin, *The Church of Notre-Dame in Montreal: an Architectural History* (1970).

Wagner, Jonathan F., *Brothers Beyond the Sea: National Socialism in Canada* (1981).

Triggs, Stanley, Brian Young, Conrad Graham and Gilles Lauzon, *Victoria Bridge: The Vital Link* (1992).

Wasserstein, Bernard, *The Secret Lives of Trebitsch Lincoln* (1988).

Weisbord, Merrily, *The Strangest Dream: Canadian Communists, the Spy Trials and the Cold War* (1983).

Wohler, J. Patrick, *Charles de Salaberry: Soldier of the Empire, Defender of Quebec* (1984).

York, Geoffrey and Loreen Pindera, *People of the Pines: the Warriors and the Legacy of Oka* (1991).

Ziegler, Philip, *King William IV* (1971).

Index

Other Books of Historical Interest from Véhicule Press

They Were So Young:
Montrealers Remember World War II
Patricia Burns
FOREWORD BY DESMOND MORTON

Memoirs of a Less Travelled Road: A Historian's Life
Marcel Trudel
[TRANSLATED FROM THE FRENCH BY JANE BRIERLEY]

Sacred Ground on de la Savane:
Montreal's Baron de Hirsch Cemetery
Danny Kucharsky

Robert Weaver: Godfather of Canadian Literature
Elaine Kalman Naves

The Shamrock & the Shield:
An Oral History of the Irish in Montreal
Patricia Burns

Yellow-Wolf & Other Tales of the Saint Lawrence
Philippe-Joseph Aubert de Gaspé
translated from the french by jane brierley

Montreal of Yesterday
Jewish Life in Montreal 1900-1920
Israel Medres
[TRANSLATED FROM THE YIDDISH BY VIVIAN FELSEN]

A Jewel in a Park: Westmount Public Library 1897-1918
Elizabeth Ida Hanson

Véhicule Press